# Questions From a Hat

*Answering the Tough Questions of Student Ministry*

NOAH RAULERSON

WESTBOW
P R E S S®
A DIVISION OF THOMAS NELSON
& ZONDERVAN

Scripture taken from the Holy Bible, NEW INTERNATIONAL VERSION®. Copyright © 1973, 1978, 1984, 2011 by Biblica, Inc. All rights reserved worldwide. Used by permission. NEW INTERNATIONAL VERSION® and NIV® are registered trademarks of Biblica, Inc. Use of either trademark for the offering of goods or services requires the prior written consent of Biblica US, Inc.

WestBow Press books may be ordered through booksellers or by contacting:

WestBow Press
A Division of Thomas Nelson & Zondervan
1663 Liberty Drive
Bloomington, IN 47403
www.westbowpress.com
1 (866) 928-1240

Because of the dynamic nature of the Internet, any web addresses or links contained in this book may have changed since publication and may no longer be valid. The views expressed in this work are solely those of the author and do not necessarily reflect the views of the publisher, and the publisher hereby disclaims any responsibility for them.

Any people depicted in stock imagery provided by Thinkstock are models, and such images are being used for illustrative purposes only. Certain stock imagery © Thinkstock.

ISBN: 978-1-5127-4575-7 (sc)
ISBN: 978-1-5127-4576-4 (hc)
ISBN: 978-1-5127-4574-0 (e)

Library of Congress Control Number: 2016909844

Print information available on the last page.

WestBow Press rev. date: 08/29/2016

# CONTENTS

# PREFACE

Before reading, you should know how this project came to be and the factors that led to this work. My journey as a Christ follower and as an author is as follows:

I can't recall a time in my life when I have not been intrigued by God. The whole idea of a being responsible for the creation of everything astounded me. From an eternal, personal mind came everything; time and space, the universe as we know it created from the words of an intelligence far beyond anyone's comprehension. What really amazes me is that this God would interact with his creation and choose to reveal himself to people. Before I go any further, it would help you to know I am one of those people fascinated by the written word. People often look at me like I am from another planet when I tell them my favorite hobby is reading. So, you can probably guess as soon as I learned to read I would eagerly and frantically search the Scriptures to learn more about this God. I would open my Bible as a child with the same fervor another child would have opening a birthday or Christmas present! Before I could read my parents had taught me that the Bible was God's Word and because it came from God it was total truth. I learned about this God as much as a six-year-old mind could comprehend. About this time I made a decision to follow Christ and get baptized. Although according to my pastor at the time, I could recite the Romans Road and answer all the right questions about salvation, the decision did not produce the kind of life change the Gospel brings. Instead of relying on Christ for my assurance and peace, I essentially became what I call an "Elementary School Pharisee." I became a legalist, desiring to be justified by my works instead of the imputed righteousness of Christ. I was the kind of kid who would serve as the "morality police" to my friends (yeah, I was *that* kid) while unaware of my own shortcomings. Thankfully through God's grace and further study of the Bible, I came across a passage of Scripture that wreaked havoc on my (now in the fourth grade) life. The passage in Galatians described my life as Paul recounts his testimony before he came to saving knowledge of Christ:

"I was advancing in Judaism beyond many of my own age among my people and was extremely zealous for the traditions of my fathers (Galatians.1:14)."

What an uncanny resemblance to my young life! There I was winning Bible drills and memory verse contests, taking attendance in Sunday school, and quoting the Bible on the school playground while entirely missing the point. I was extremely zealous for the Bible but missed its main theme. I was zealous for church traditions without knowing the reasons behind them. I was zealous for God but never met him. Paul could not find salvation in mere zeal for the law and neither could I. Just three days shy of my tenth birthday on February 22, 1995; I gave my life to Christ. I recognized him for who he is, not only my Savior but as my Lord. My life I now live for him. No longer do I do "good things" out of fear of breaking the Law, but out of love and gratitude for Jesus who held nothing back from me. The things that I *had to do* before I met Jesus were now the things I *got to do.*

As much as I enjoy reading, I never felt the desire to write a book. The daunting task of organizing and compiling my jumbled, scatter-brained thoughts petrified me to no end. However, I have learned that God will use some of the most unqualified folks to do things for the kingdom. No greater evidence of this in my own life as I finished my senior year of high school. Although I had lived a season of rebellion during my final year as high school student, I was still active in church. During this season of my life I felt a call to full time ministry. At a summer camp that year I surrendered to that call which set in motion events that led to many years of theological and ministerial training at two academic institutions. As I neared the end of my time at seminary, the time came for me to become an ordained minister. For those of you unfamiliar with this process, when the time comes for a person called into ministry to become ordained, this person meets with the pastors and deacons/ elders from a local church and is questioned. My home church, First Baptist Church of Callahan, Florida oversaw my ordination process. Again, for those unfamiliar with this process, the church needs to know if a candidate meets the qualifications to be set apart (ordained) for ministry. In my experience, I was questioned on fundamental doctrines (God, Jesus, the Bible, salvation) my philosophy of ministry, and how I planned to serve as a pastor. At this point, a deacon named Blake asked me a question that would serve as the foundation for this book: "As someone going into Christian ministry, what is your biggest concern for churches these days?" Without hesitation I responded with these two words: Biblical Illiteracy.

Every Sunday, people fill the pews of churches having little to no understanding of the Bible. There are various reasons as to why this happens. Some people simply do not read their Bibles... ever. These are the ones who usually don't even carry their Bibles to church and pray that the text for that Sunday will be projected on a screen behind the pulpit. Some read their Bibles when they come to church, but leave them unopened at their homes. There are some people who genuinely desire to read their Bibles and learn more about God, but simply don't know how for whatever reason (unable to find a reading plan, struggling readers, etc.). Sadly, some people struggle to understand the Bible because they view it as fragmented, unrelated stories instead of one grand narrative. From Genesis to Revelation, the Bible tells one story: redemption.

On the other hand, there are some people in church that faithfully study the Bible, but are still left with tough questions. If this is you, don't worry. You are not alone. I am with you. Your pastor is with you. The greatest theologians that ever lived are with you. Learning more about the Bible is part of the sanctification process as believers. We grow in our faith by doing so. In fact, it is impossible to mature in the faith without studying the Bible. However, you never stop learning. We as humans will never fully understand everything about an infinite God in our finite minds. The Bible offers a stark reminder that "...the secret things belong the Lord (Deuteronomy 29:29)." While these words are inspired and true, this passage is not an invitation to give up the study of the Bible nor is it an excuse for intellectual laziness. The Christian faith, both simplistic and complex, should never be approached with a haphazard intellectual attitude. I can recall a particular occasion where I was sharing my faith to a person on a college campus. At the end of the discussion the person told me that he could not accept the Christian faith because doing so would be committing "intellectual suicide." To this person, logic, reason, science, and facts would have to be discarded in order to believe in Christ. This could not be any further from the truth. Faith and reason are not enemies, but rather work in harmony to point people to the truth.

This book is presented in a question and answer format not by accident. These are real questions from real students. As a student minister, I have served in several churches and in multiple events where these questions were asked. Middle and high school students are inquisitive by nature, so it is no surprise they are also curious about spiritual matters. Sadly, many of these students asking these questions have little to no understanding of who God is, that Jesus died to pay the penalty for their sins and desires to have a relationship with them. Why? Their parents have intentionally or unintentionally ignored Deuteronomy 6:4-9. In this passage, the parents in the nation of Israel are instructed to teach the commands of God to their children. This was to be foundational for living and the precedence for their very livelihood. Look at the importance God places on instruction of his word:

"Hear, O Israel: The Lord our God, the Lord is one. Love the Lord your God with all your heart and with all your soul and with all your strength. These commandments that I give you today are to be on your hearts. Impress them on your children. Talk about them when you sit at home and when you walk along the road, when you lie down and when you get up. Tie them as symbols on your hands and bind them on your foreheads. Write them on the doorframes of your houses and on your gates (Deut. 6:4-9)."

For children in this environment, learning about God would have been as natural as breathing. Unfortunately, many believers today do not place the same importance on theological training. Some parents consistently place other activities before the things of God then are bewildered as to why their children are spiritually confused. Some parents faithfully teach the Scriptures to their children and place it as top priority. These parents are superheroes in the faith and have my utmost respect. Other parents may have a strong desire to teach the Bible to their children, but may not know how. For those parents, I hope this book can serve as one of many tools to assist you.

The reasons for this book are not anything new or out of the ordinary. My desire is to equip students, their parents, and youth ministry leaders with a quick reference tool to help answer questions that may arise when studying the Bible. Some of these topics are fundamental teachings that are not up for debate, while others are not so cut and dry. This book will provide encouragement and reinforcement of your beliefs, but may also convict and correct some misconceptions you have. For the Christian, devoting oneself as best as possible to the study of Scripture is not an option. The stakes are too high. Our churches, by not passing the torch as they should have, are in danger of raising up the most Bible-illiterate generation in modern history. This can't happen. Our churches desperately need strong Christians capable of sharing their faith with non-Christians and discipling other Christians. Let us echo Peter who encouraged believers to " ...in your hearts revere Christ as Lord. Always be prepared to give an answer to everyone who asks you to give the reason for the hope that you have. But do this with gentleness and respect (1 Peter 3:15)." In other words, share your faith. However, you can't share what you don't know. Let's embark on the journey together, that God may find in us a faithful servant.

A few final thoughts before you go any further:

1. Merely accepting knowledge into your head as fact is not enough to foster life change. The truths of Scripture must penetrate your heart as well as your mind. James 1:22–25 warns believers not to merely listen to the Word, but put

what is heard into action and apply it to daily living. In other words, ethics is applied theology. What one does is indicative of what one believes.

2. Although this book will cover a variety of topics, it is by no means exhaustive. In some cases answering a question may produce other questions. Nor is this a heavy, academic endeavor. Most of the references within are from the Bible itself. However, over the course of writing this book several extra-biblical sources were used that will be listed in a works consulted page. I strongly recommend consulting this list for further reading and study.

3. The title and inspiration from this book comes from an event done several times a year in the student ministry where I serve as associate pastor/minister of students. Aptly dubbed "Questions from a Hat," students write their anonymous questions on an index card, fold it, and then drop it in a hat. Questions are pulled at random and discussed with the group. I can honestly attest these are some of the best nights within the student ministry.

4. All Scripture quoted is from the NIV unless otherwise noted.

# CHAPTER 1

# CREATION

### Who Wrote Genesis, and How Did the Author Know the Story of Creation?

Authorship of the book of Genesis is generally attributed to Moses. The first five books of the Old Testament—Genesis, Exodus, Leviticus, Numbers, and Deuteronomy—are known as the Pentateuch, which is also believed to been authored by Moses. However, this presents a problem for many, since the time period in which Moses lived was far removed from the events of creation. It is likely that Moses compiled the creation account from various sources passed down throughout the years between the life of Adam and his own life many years later. The Bible does not provide an exact time about when writing methods were implemented, but it is safe to assume that the creation account was passed from Adam and his sons orally for generations until methods of writing and recording data were invented. In our modern society, the notion of oral transmission of events over generations is difficult for us to understand. In today's world, information is shared worldwide at the click of a button. However, in the ancient world, passing on an oral tradition was the norm. Even after methods of writing were invented, languages were still being formed (especially after the events of the Tower of Babel) and many of the world's peoples remained illiterate. Even later during Jesus's time, the process of writing and copying material was a time-consuming, expensive endeavor, and it made reading and writing mostly exclusive to the wealthy and educated. Not until the invention of the printing press by Johannes Guttenberg in 1440 was copying made easier and less expensive. Even in 2015, illiteracy rates around the world still remain high, while some cultures around the globe do not maintain a written language. Thus, even in the digital age, many people around the world still rely on the spoken word to pass on the events of their culture to the next generation. So it shouldn't be hard for us to fathom stories passed down orally for generations.

## If God Created the Universe, Then Who Created God?

No one created God. Nor did God create himself (what an absurd notion that something that doesn't exist could create itself). The first four words of the Bible found in Genesis 1:1 answer this question: "In the beginning, God ..." These four words are so loaded with meaning that it boggles the mind. Yet the concept of an eternal, everlasting God is quite overlooked in this passage. God has always existed. He is outside of time and space. Therefore, it is impossible for God to be a created being. He is eternal, with no beginning and no end. Try to think of time and space (the universe) as many dominoes stacked on their sides, ready for someone to push the first domino and begin a chain reaction that will eventually knock down the rest. The falling dominoes cannot start the sequence by themselves. A force outside and beyond the dominoes must begin the process. Just as a child begins the process with the dominoes with a flick of the finger, God is the first "mover" of the universe. If someone or something had created God, then that would make God less than who he is. The Bible teaches that God has always been and always will be (1 Timothy 1:17; Revelation 1:8, 21:6, 22:13). When we mention God, we need to keep in mind that He is the triune God: Father, Son, and Holy Spirit. This is why Jesus could claim to have always existed (John 8:58). John the apostle also testified to the eternality of Christ (John 1:1), and Paul taught that all things were made by and through Jesus (Colossians 1:15–18). Micah, an Old Testament prophet, also wrote that the Messiah's (Jesus's) works are eternal (Micah 5:2).

## How Did God Create People?

This is an excellent question, and it must be answered twofold. Essentially, man was created in God's image and from the ground (with women coming from the man in a slightly different way). According to the creation account in Genesis 1:26–28, God created man in his own image. This is often referred to as the *Imago Dei,* the Latin phrase translated as "God's image." Humans hold a distinct and special place in the created order. Nothing else in creation bears the Imago Dei. But what does this mean? In the verses closing out the opening chapter of Genesis, humans are given two commands: reproduce, and take care the earth. Creating is one way in which humans share God's image. God gives humans the ability to partake in creation. This is done by reproducing the human race and by serving as stewards, or caretakers, of the environment. Men and women create every day by producing beautiful babies and by sustaining the world around them. Humans have the intelligence to use natural resources to invent, manipulate, and restore the environment. While some animals can build and organize (birds, ants, beavers, etc.) humans are far superior and unique in the manner by which they interact with the world. Isn't it truly great that God gives humans the chance to partake in the creation and stewardship of his work? Now, don't go puffing your ego too much here. Humans can only manipulate what God has given in the first place. God created *ex nihilo*, which means "out of nothing." God spoke into absolutely nothing and created everything—well almost everything.

Humans are also distinct in the created order in that we are the only beings made from creation itself. Man and woman were not made out of nothing. Keep in mind that the second chapter of Genesis is a commentary on the first. In other words, Genesis 2 provides the reader with more details of the creation timeline described in Genesis 1. Thus, the reader is exposed to the details of the creation of man in Genesis 2:7. Rather than to create man *ex nihilo*, man was formed from the dust of the ground, and God breathed life into him at that point. The wording here in the original language suggests this "breath of life" as intimacy with God through this creation process. Thus, man is more unique and intimate with God than other parts of creation. Also, the phrase "living being" tells the reader that humans have a spiritual aspect to their makeup. Not only is man a physical and emotional being. We as humans possess a spirit that will live on after the physical body has ceased to function. The same applies for the woman, although woman was created out of the rib of man as recorded in Genesis 2:21–23. Although the mode by which God chose to create the woman may seem farfetched and strange to us today, let's keep in mind that this showcases man and woman's similarity both sexually and socially. They are similar, but different. Even so, their differences are meant to complement one another, thus we have what is called *complementary difference*. What does this mean? Think how this works with a hammer and nails. Both are tools designed differently but for similar purposes, and are used to work together to achieve a goal. For someone trying to build something, having an abundance of just one of these does not work. They are meant to work together. Men and women work together to fulfill the commands found in Genesis 1 to reproduce the human race and to take care of the environment God created.

## Where Did Cain Find His Wife?

This question is a Sunday school classic, to say the least. The answer is not simple, as the Bible does not inform the reader who she is or where she came from, only that Cain had a wife. However, we must keep in mind that the author is not attempting to give a detailed genealogy in this passage, but rather he is attempting to explain the tragic consequences of Cain's decision to murder his brother, Abel. With this in mind, there are two possible scenarios that help us to solve this mystery. Both have their problems in that each of them present arguments from silence. Personally, I do not have a problem with someone holding to either one of these views. The account of Cain after the murder of Abel is found in Genesis 4:15–24.

Many scholars speculate that Cain's wife was one of his sisters. Genesis 5:3–4 informs the reader that Adam had many sons and daughters during his lifetime. It is quite possible that Cain took one of his sisters to be his wife. While this act is certainly reprehensible in the modern society, it was a common practice in the ancient world. Abraham and Sarah were half siblings according to Genesis 20:12, with both having the same father. Also, we must keep in mind that in addition to close family marriages, polygamy was also practiced early in the book of Genesis. Lamech, the son of Cain, had at least two wives at some point in his life (Genesis 4:19). It is interesting to note that polygamy is seen so early in human history, Lamech being only Adam's grandson and the third generation of the human race. With men taking more than one wife and producing multiple offspring, the relations become more distant over time. In fact, prohibitions against marriage of close family members do not appear until the Law of Moses, although the account of Lot and his daughters (Genesis 19:30–36) is recorded in a negative manner.

The other theory states other humans were created during the creation account. Some scholars believe the plural pronoun "them" found in Genesis 1:26–29 and 5:1–2 implies multiple people rather than just one male (Adam) and one female (Eve). It is also interesting to note that Cain took a wife for himself after he departed from Eden and settled in Nod (Genesis 4:16–17). Historians note the order of events here and speculate that Cain found a wife in Nod, but do not rule out the possibility than Cain may have taken a sister as his wife with him to Nod. Either way, this view is problematic in that it leaves us with more questions than answers. No matter which option one chooses here, we need to keep in mind the Bible does not provide a definitive answer as to the origins of Cain's wife.

## Does the Bible Mention Dinosaurs?

The word "dinosaur" never occurs in Scripture nor is there a mention of them during the creation story or the flood. Therefore any mention of dinosaurs in the Bible is speculative considering the Bible does not provide the answer outright. However, the recent findings of fossils proving the existence of these animals shows us that God did in fact create these now extinct creatures. The short answer: we really don't know. But since this is a book where the author is asked a question and gets to offer his take on the subject when the Bible is unclear, here it goes.

There are passages in the book of Job that have led some to speculate that dinosaurs may have been on the earth during the time of Job. Placing Job in the timeline of human history is a widely debated task among scholars but most agree that Job should be placed somewhere in early Genesis. Therein lies the bigger problem: did the events in Job take place before or after the flood? There is no way to know. Why is this important? The timing of Job either pre-flood or post-flood would be helpful in answering the question of whether dinosaurs were on the ark or had gone extinct by the time Noah completed the ark. Again, a speculative answer to a question just leads to more speculation.

What are these passages in Job that could be possibly talking about dinosaurs? Job 41 mentions a "Leviathan," a fearsome sea creature that is said to had limbs, scaly, thick skin, "shields" on its back, and breath of fire (sounds almost like a dragon than a dinosaur!). The author of Job describes this creature having vast strength and power. Although this creature cannot be identified, its description is unlike any animal found in the oceans today. Also, in Job 40:15–24 the word "Behemoth" is used to describe a massive land creature. This animal is said to have legs like rods of iron, a tail like a cedar tree, a large frame, and feeds off grass and vegetation. Some have speculated elephants or rhinos here, but I've never seen one with the tail like a cedar tree (Job 40:17). Even the most casual dinosaur enthusiast can picture a Brontosaurus or Brachiosaurus (long-necked dinosaurs) here given the description.

Although it is fun to speculate, there is no way to be certain what is described here. However, it seems very likely given these descriptions that at least some species of dinosaur were alive in the early Genesis period when Job lived.

# CHAPTER 2

# GOD & MAN

### If God Knew Humans Were Going to Sin, Why Did He Create Us in the First Place?

This is an interesting question considering what we know about God. In order to explore this mystery, we must look at God's character and his feelings toward sin. The Bible is abundantly clear concerning God's feelings to sin: he abhors it (Psalms 5:4–6), hates it (Psalms 11:5–7, 45:6), and will not allow it to go unpunished (Hosea 9:15; Amos 6:8; Matthew 23). In fact, a major theme in the Minor Prophets (those small books in the back of the Old Testament that receive far less attention than they ought) is God's attitude towards sin and his claims to punish sinful nations. On the other hand, God is not only just but also loving and gracious. While humans sin continually, the Bible reveals that he loves people (Matthew 23:37; John 3:16; Romans 5:8; 1 John 3:1) and desires to have a relationship with them. Though God hates sin because he is holy and perfect (Psalms 22:3; Isaiah 6:1–5, 40:25; Matthew 5:48), Scripture tells us God is slow to anger and compassionate (Nehemiah 9:17; Psalms 103:8; Jonah 4:2; Nahum 1:3). Also, let us not forget that God sought Adam and Eve while they hid in shame (Genesis 3:8–9) and spared the wicked city of Nineveh (Jonah 3:10). In fact, the plan of redemption exists in the mind of God and therefore timeless. Peter and John both teach in their writings that redemption was planned before creation and time began (1 Peter 1:18–20; Revelation 13:8).

Perhaps the best explanation for God creating humanity is his relational nature. I am sure you have heard in church at some point that God created humans out of boredom and loneliness. The notion that an omnipotent God, needing nothing outside of himself to sustain his existence got bored is utterly ridiculous. God did not need us. Remember that the God of the Bible is Trinitarian in nature: the Father, Son, and Spirit (commonly referred to as the Godhead). The three distinct members of the Trinity were in perfect harmony and relation with each other before time began. Not only is God relational towards man, man was created to give God glory as we reflect him and were created in his image (Genesis 1:26–27; Ecclesiastes 7:29). Essentially, humanity was created in order to reflect God's image and to maintain our relationship with him. By doing these two, we fulfill our ultimate purpose as created beings: to give God glory.

This is where my limits as a theologian end. The Bible tells us that God is love and loves perfectly (1 John 4:8), but I cannot comprehend the depths of his love. From our beginning, humans have taken up arms in rebellion against God. We have tried to be like him in attempts to usurp his authority and power. We have shaken our fists in defiance as he has revealed his character to us. When God chose to reveal himself most plainly and vividly through the person of Jesus Christ, God in the flesh, we murdered him. Though we rejected, mocked, and murdered him, Christ now sits at the right hand of the Father serving as our advocate (1 John

2:1–2) and High Priest (Hebrews 4:14). Clearly God loves us. You may question why he should but cannot question that he does.

### If God Hates Sin So Much, Why Didn't He Create Us Perfect From the Start?

This question is similar to the last, but here we must approach the creation of man from a different angle. Humans are indeed sinful, but are we free beings with the choice to sin? The answer is yes, and the book of Genesis tells us that man chose sin early and with relative ease. Try to imagine a world free from the choice to sin. Paul writes in the book of Romans not only humans but also the entire created order suffers from the effects of sin (Romans 8:19–24). The notion of a world free from the effects of sin sounds good, does it not? This world would have no death, disease, violence, famine, or war, therefore suffering and pain would be nonexistent. In this world, no more children would be killed by the stupidity of a drunk driver and would also be free of radiation and chemotherapy treatments. Such a world would be free of sexual abuse, divorce, affairs, rape, and STD's. One could almost get lost imagining the bliss of such world. Sadly, this is not the world that exists today. In case you haven't noticed, the world is a fallen place full of desperation and despair. Ungodliness lurks around the street corners and in the recesses of our own hearts. The Bible tells us the humanity is sinful and sin comes as natural to us as breathing (Psalms 51:5; Isaiah 53:6, 64:6; Jeremiah 17:9; Romans 3:10, 23).

However, the question remains why God would create and allow such a world. We need to be careful here as we continue: this is not God's fault. Sin comes from man. When God finished his creation, he said it was "very good" (Genesis 1:31) even after the creation of man. Some argue that because God knew that man would sin he had to have caused it to happen, since nothing happens without God's permission or knowledge. While it is correct and logical that God allowed sin to happen, we must be careful not to confuse *predestination* with *foreknowledge.* To know something in advance and to actually cause something to happen are two different concepts. If God caused Adam to sin, then God would be the author of evil, which is totally absurd and outside his character. The only logical conclusion is that God created man with some degree of free will. C.S. Lewis argues in the second chapter his book, *The Problem of Pain,* a world without pain and suffering caused by man's free will (and his choice to sin) is an illogical world and thus could not be created by God. While God is omnipotent, he cannot do the illogical or nonsensical since he is the author of all logic and reason. Therefore, we must conclude that humans have a free will and choose to sin.

Although by man's free will sin entered the created order, the freedom to choose is a gift to mankind from God and it does not compromise God's sovereignty in the least. Imagine if you didn't have free will and God created you to love him and serve him with no choice in the matter. What kind of relationship would that be? When one examines Scripture, we see God revealing himself to people and offering a chance for humans to repent. Isaiah, speaking for God offers a clear example of this: "Come let us reason together, though your sins are like scarlet, they shall be as white as snow (Isaiah1:18)." In fact, Jesus' earthly ministry was characterized by offers of repentance and following him (Matthew 3:12, 4:19, 9:19; Mark 8:34; Luke 9:23, 59; John 8:12). Furthermore, if God is the one who created us with our ability to choose how does that take away from his sovereignty? It was his choice to create us that way and does not make him any less powerful. Our sin did not take him by surprise or leave him without a plan. The plan of redemption has always been in place and by his grace we can come to Christ in repentance, by grace through faith.

## If God Wants Us to Believe Him, Why Doesn't He Show Himself?

He has. Paul addresses this issue in the opening chapter of the book of Romans. He states that because God created the universe and all that is in it, including man, that we are accountable to him and have no excuse for not believing in him. Furthermore, Paul argues mankind early in history knew God by observation of the created order, but rejected him because of their sinful nature and desire for idols (Romans 1:18–25). Essentially, what Paul is saying is because God created everything that we observe we in turn cannot deny his existence. This teaching is what theologians call **general revelation:** the idea that God reveals himself to all humanity through his creation. I challenge you to take a look through the Psalms; they are filled with invitations to the reader to examine nature and reflect on the glory of God (Psalm 19 is a great example). Think of general revelation this way: when a famous painter finishes a masterpiece, there are certain qualities and characteristics that make the painting unique to its painter. Likewise, music can oftentimes be identified with a certain band or musician by qualities found within, such as tempo and key. The art will reflect the artist. The universe is God's handiwork; its beauty and complexity reflect his nature and character. This is why the man on the island who has never heard the name of Jesus is still accountable to God as Paul reminds us that he is without excuse (Romans 1:20).

God's revelation to man doesn't stop there, however. Take comfort and assurance in the words of the author of Hebrews: "In the past God spoke to our ancestors through the prophets at many times and in various ways, but in these last days he has spoken to us by his Son, whom he appointed heir of all things, and through whom also he made the universe. The Son is the radiance of God's glory and the exact representation of his being, sustaining all things by his powerful word. After he had provided purification for sins, he sat down at the right hand of the Majesty in heaven (Hebrews 1:1-3)." Here we learn that God spoke through people in the Old Testament such as Moses, Isaiah, and Jeremiah but God's final word and authority for us is Jesus. In Jesus, we have all we need to hear. God does not need to speak anymore (like he did with the prophets) because Jesus and the his inspiration on the writers of the New Testament provides humanity with what they need to know for salvation and Christian living. The Holy Spirit leads and guides the believer as he/she studies the Scripture, which is the ultimate authority for the Christian. Jesus and the Scriptures provide humanity with what theologians call **special revelation.** While general revelation communicates God to mankind through creation and our conscience, special revelation provides specific information on God, man, sin, redemption, and the Gospel.

An agnostic once told me that if he died and could ask God anything, he would ask him why he didn't make himself known. I responded that God did show himself...God gave this person nature, his word, and his Son. God has gone through great lengths to bring this man to him. If one is seeking God, he isn't that hard to find.

# How Did People in the Old Testament Get Saved?

This is a good question. If salvation is based on Christ (1 Corinthians 15:1–4), how did people come to salvation thousands of years before the Jesus's death on the cross? How did the Gospel effect David, Joshua, Ruth, Rahab, and countless others? We feel certain it did as the author of Hebrews compiled the aptly dubbed "Hall of Faith" (Hebrews 11), providing the reader full assurance that these Old Testament saints were now with God. But how can this be so if Jesus had not come and completed his work? A study of salvation and redemption must be done and it starts in Genesis.

It is both alarming and disappointing how many believers in churches today avoid the Old Testament. You don't have to search churches long before you find someone who claims they are not concerned with the Old Testament because it is full of wrath, war, animal sacrifice, rituals, curses, death, no grace, and unpronounceable names (OK, I'll give you the last one). People who think this way argue the New Testament is all grace and the Old Testament is all punishment and wrath. Both of those statements are incorrect. These folks will cling to the New Testament and avoid the Old Testament due to fear, anxiety, or merely a lack of understanding of its main themes. The main theme of the Old Testament is **the promise of redemption from sin by the Messiah**. The word "Messiah" means, "chosen or anointed one"; someone who would come and right all the wrongs of sin and undo the curse of sin. Due to sin entering the world through Adam, God would now make a way to reconcile man unto himself. He promised Adam and Eve redemption right after the fall of man (Genesis 3:15), assuring Eve that one of her descendants would conquer sin, death, and Satan (the serpent). This is the first mention of the Gospel

15

as this descendant who would come is the Messiah, Jesus Christ. Remember, the Bible tells us that Jesus is the lamb slain before the foundation of the world so redemption has been in place in the mind of God since eternity past (1 Peter 1:20).

To understand how people were saved in the Old Testament however we must look at the life of Abraham. As Abraham entered in relationship with God, the author of the book of Genesis makes a very interesting statement in Genesis 15:6, "And Abraham believed God, and it was accounted to him for righteousness." In the Hebrew language, the word for righteousness carries the meaning "to be in right standing"; it is a legal term. For example, if someone committed a crime and subsequently paid the fine attached or served the allotted prison sentence, the judge would declare them to be in right standing and free to go. The person would be declared to be back in good standing or favor with the state and not be seen as a prisoner or criminal anymore. Therefore, because he was declared righteous, Abraham was in good standing with God. His relationship with the Lord was cemented in this right standing because of his belief. Abraham believed God's promises, put his faith in God and was declared righteous, or what we would call today ... saved! One would be inclined to ask what promises Abraham believed that made him righteous. Yes, Abraham believed that God would bless him materially and make him the father not only of Isaac but also of the nation of Israel. Those promises were good, but the ones that apply here are the Messianic promises, or the ones dealing with the coming of Jesus. God promised Abraham that the Messiah would be one of his descendants and that all the nations of the world would be blessed through this Messiah (Genesis 12:3, 18:17–18; Matthew 1:1). Paul addresses this very issue in Romans 4 where he actually quotes Genesis 15:6 in order to explain to believers in Rome that **salvation**

**has always been by grace, through faith, in the promises of God.** Peter also addressed this question by asserting the prophets in the Old Testament spoke of things in their day that Jesus fulfilled (1 Peter 1:10-12). Peter says the Old Testament prophets preached the Gospel long before Jesus was born in Bethlehem! In other words, Abraham and other Old Testament people believed in the Messiah (Jesus) looking forward to the promise. In contrast, we as New Testament saints believe in God's promises by looking back to Jesus on the cross (2 Corinthians 5:21).

## If Old Testament People Were Saved by Grace Through Faith in the Messiah, Why Did God Command Animal Sacrifices?

In the previous question we learned that no one was saved by animal sacrifices. So why did God command the Old Testament believers to sacrifice animals? A quick look through the Pentateuch (Genesis–Deuteronomy) shows a plethora of detailed instructions on the consistent sacrifices of animals for covering of the people's sin. We must remember that sin is destructive, costly, and eventually results in death (both physically and spiritually). Paul clearly stated the penalty for sin is death (Romans 6:23). Likewise James in his epistle reminds his readers that death is the end result of sinful thoughts and actions (James 1:13–15). Death happened as a result of sin. God was the one who sacrificed the animals to provide skins to cover Adam and Eve after they fell into sin in Genesis 3. The entirety of the Old Testament was a foreshadowing and precursor to Christ. Jesus is the ultimate payment for sin. His death on the cross paid for the sin of the world. In fact, in the Old Testament the priests would lay their hands on the animals symbolizing the sin of the people being laid upon the animal. When Jesus died on the cross he took the sin of the entire world on himself. In short, God instituted the animal sacrifices because Jesus had not come yet and the people needed constant visual reminder of the consequences of sin. Sacrifices in the Old Testament were merely a foreshadowing and thus fulfilled in the sacrifice of Jesus on the cross. As Christians, we offer up the sacrifice of our lives and ourselves to Jesus as an act of worship (Romans 12:1–2).

## What Can We Do to Make God the Number One Priority in Our Lives?

Prioritizing God as the most important aspect your life is perhaps the center of Christian living. Placing God as Lord of all and dying to yourself, your wants, and accepting whatever God desires for your life is all part of the sanctification process; looking like Jesus more each day. Although this is foundational and seems like a no-brainer for the Christian it is hard to maintain because of our fallen nature. It takes discipline for us to place God as the center of our busy lives. Not only are our lives oftentimes too busy, we as humans are constantly trying to put someone or something on the throne of our lives (without even realizing what we're doing). This teaching is called the **Lordship of Christ,** meaning that Jesus must be calling the shots in your life, and is emphasized in my teachings as a youth pastor. Most teens (like most adults) are content with belief in God and casual church attendance, but either have no desire or are unable to make God the number priority in their lives. There is a very powerful biblical passage that focuses on some practical ways to make sure Christ is prioritized in the life of the believer.

Perhaps Paul said it best when he penned Romans 12:1-2 "Therefore, I urge you, brothers and sisters, in view of God's mercy, to offer your bodies as a living sacrifice, holy and pleasing to God—this is your true and proper worship. Do not conform to the pattern of this world, but be transformed by the renewing of your mind. Then you will be able to test and approve what God's will is—his good, pleasing and perfect will."

According to Paul, giving God proper lordship in our lives requires sacrifice. Our lives are to be an offering. Many Christians today come to God and claim to offer their lives only to later start taking it back one decision at a time. These people compromise in one area of their live, then another and another until it is not God calling the shots in their lives, but rather themselves. Paul's words here are in stark contrast to today's cultural Christianity wherein people want all the blessings without any of the costs. Like most things, the kingdom of God is only worth to someone what they are willing to pay. The kingdom is costly, as is following God. The more you follow God the more likely you will be faced with giving up your wants, desires, comforts, and security for the sake of the Gospel. That's why the old hymn is titled *I Surrender All* rather than *I Surrender Some*. Which song are you singing?

Paul also gives three verbal commands in this passage that drive home his point. First off, he warns not to **conform** to the world. Many Christians have a tendency to be worldly; we all do given our sin nature. The world is fun and sin is enjoyable for a season. Perhaps it is not a decadent lifestyle of sin that is tempting but rather a cold, complacent, inactive faith that draws the believer away from the Lord. Regardless, Paul warns not to conform (meaning to share similarities and obedience) to the ungodly world. Rather, in his second command Paul urges the believer be **transformed**. When a person becomes a Christian that person should undergo a total transformation. The old person and the sinful attitudes and actions are now laid at the foot of the cross. Therefore, the life of the Christian should not be similar to the old, sinful person. Yes, Christians will continue to struggle with sin given our sin nature and the overall wickedness of the human heart. The key factor here is consistency. Does the life of the believer exemplify continual, consistent sin or the process of sanctification? Despite our continued sin Christ is still gracious and forgiving as long as we are repentant. Finally, Paul urges to believers to **renew** their mind. Dying to one's self, not adapting to the world, making God boss of your life; it is all a daily process. Every day the believer must make a conscious and deliberate decision to continue to follow Christ or to fall back in their former lifestyle.

## Was Jesus Dying on the Cross Really the Only Way to Save Us?

Absolutely. Remember that Jesus is the "lamb slain before the foundation of the world (Revelation 13:8)," meaning the plan for salvation has been in place before creation. The plan for Jesus to die on the cross as the payment for the sins of humanity has been in place in the mind of God long before any of us were around. Sin did not take God by surprise when man rebelled against him. However, sin is a big deal...the biggest deal. The book of Romans tells us the penalty for sin is death. The death here is not just physical death but spiritual death meaning an eternity separated from God's presence, grace, and mercy (Romans 3:23; 6:23). Due to the destructive nature of sin, it separates us from God. God is holy and therefore cannot tolerate sin or allow sin into his presence. This leaves one to ponder how a sinful man enters into a relationship (and eventually heaven) with a holy and perfect God. In the Old Testament, believers would sacrifice animals as a symbolic, yet temporary foreshadowing of the ultimate sacrifice who was to come: Jesus. Like the animals of the Old Testament that had to be without defect or flaw, this new sacrifice would have to unblemished, meaning the sacrifice would have to be perfect, unblemished, and sinless (Hebrews 10:1–18). Jesus is the Lamb. John the Baptist referred to Jesus as the lamb who would remove our sin debt (John 1:29). Jesus was the sacrifice to take away our sins. Paul wrote the following when discussing Jesus' work on the cross "God made Him who had no sin to be sin for us, so that in him we might become the righteousness of God (2 Corinthians. 5:21)." That is how an imperfect man enters into fellowship with a holy God. Therefore, God sees not the sin and wickedness of the Christian, but rather the holiness and righteousness of Jesus.

Now that we've established Jesus is the way to heaven let's be sure to understand he is the only way (John 14:6). If there were any other way to redeem sinful man, God would have pursued that route instead of putting on flesh and dying a cruel death on a Roman cross. Jesus himself asked in a prayer if there were any other way, but nevertheless prayed for God's will to be done (Luke 22:42). I can only speculate here as to the mysteries of Jesus being both fully human and divine but it seems in his humanity Jesus prayed to be spared from what was going to happen to him in a few hours. However, Jesus knew what must be done to spare sinful man. The cross didn't take Jesus by surprise as he had predicted his death several times during his ministry (Matthew 16:21–28;Mark

9:30–32;Luke 9:22–27; John 3:14–15). Furthermore, during the last meal with his disciples Jesus offered bread and wine claiming they represented his body that would be broken and blood which would be spilled, respectively (Matthew 26–29). Considering Jesus predicted his death many times and stated outright that he was the only way to God, any other method to achieve reconciliation with God is impossible.

## How Do You Know if God is Listening to You?

The best evidence I can give to answer this question is the authority of Scriptures in which God himself, prophets, and apostles encourage people to pray. The psalmist declares God is close to those who call out to him (Psalms 145:18) and the book of Proverbs tells us God hears the prayers of those who belong to him (Proverbs 15:29). In the New Testament, Jesus teaches his followers a model prayer (Matt. 6:9–13) and set us an example by consistently retreating from the crowds to a silent place to pray to the Father (Luke 6:12). Paul taught on prayer as well, urging believers to pray continually (1 Thessalonians 5:17), to make requests to God (Philippians 4:8), and that the Holy Spirit would help us to pray (Romans 8:26). James told the recipients of his letters that continual prayer of the righteous did much good (James 5:16). With these verses just scratching the surface of what the Bible teaches on prayer, it is certain that God hears the prayers of his people.

Read the last sentence again and pay close attention. God hears his people. The aforementioned verses in Proverbs and James tell us God hears the prayer of the righteous. The righteous in scripture are those who are in fellowship with God, part of God's family. In other words for us today: Christians. There are many theologians who believe in light of these Scriptures God does not listen to the prayers of the unrepentant until they pray to become a Christian. While biblical evidence for this is minimal I do believe the logic to be sound.

Many teenagers I counsel do not have an active prayer life or if they do they pray for the wrong things. For example, prayers for trucks, a significant other, good grades (despite poor study habits) would be examples of praying amiss. The book of James warns us about praying for the wrong things, praying in an unwise manner, or praying selfishly (James 4:3). I encourage people I am around (and myself) to pray in such a way that would be honorable. Yes, pray for your needs but do not neglect praying for the needs of others. Your needs and the needs of others aren't always physical, either. Pray that you and those you sit with in church would understand Scripture. Pray for your church to be spiritually healthy. Pray that you could be a blessing to someone else. Pray for the lost. Pray that those across the street and across the world would come to know Christ as savior. Pray that you could be part of that. If you pray in a manner such as this you can be sure that God is listening. You are praying to be part of his agenda and that blesses the heart of our Lord.

If you are like me you may not be the best prayer warrior. That is one area of my life which God has grown me tremendously though I still feel I need work. I have a problem stopping my tasks of the day and taking moments to communicate with God. I needed something in my life that would remind me to pray. After talking with some of my teens and parents in leadership in our church, we decided to change a storage closet in our youth area into a prayer room. The room was repainted and decorated with Scripture on the walls that reminded us to pray. Components of this room included thanksgiving, confession, repentance, supplication, and prayers for the lost. I can honestly attest this has been a tremendous blessing in my life and the lives of the students that take the time to use this prayer room. I would recommend to any person or church group to have a place like this set up. Get still. Talk to God. More importantly, listen to God. You may be surprised at what he has to say if you listen.

# CHAPTER 3

# THE BIBLE

### How Old is the Bible?

The Bible as we know it has a vast and rich history, thus this question cannot simply be answered by providing a number or a date. Nor did one man simply sit down one day and write the entire Bible from Genesis to Revelation. Many people wrote the Bible over many years on three different continents (Asia, Africa, and Europe). While the Bible names about 40 different authors, many of the historical books such as Kings and Chronicles span generations, leaving us to ascertain that they were penned by many scribes and historians over the years. The Bible begins with the Pentateuch (the first five books of the Old Testament) whose authorship is generally attributed to Moses. Believing that Moses authored Genesis through Deuteronomy, it is safe to assume he did so late in life around 1420 BC. From that point on, the Bible is clear in its historical claims following the events of Israel throughout human history. The period of Joshua and Judges lasted until about 1000 BC when David took the throne. The kingdom of Israel split shortly after Solomon's death around 931 BC. The northern kingdom of Israel fell in 729 BC to the Assyrians, and the southern kingdom of Judah was conquered by

Babylon around 586 BC. Prophets such as Daniel, Ezra, Nehemiah, Ezekiel, and Malachi wrote from this point until around 400 BC.

This point marked the end of the Old Testament period of writing and prophecy. Other works were written during this time but were found insufficient to be considered part of the Bible. These works would later be called the *Apocrypha*. Thus, this period was called "Silent Years," considering God did not speak to his people through a prophet. However, God began to speak directly to people again in the New Testament, beginning with Zachariah (and later his son, John the Baptist) and Mary who would soon be the mother of Jesus. After the death and resurrection of Jesus, his followers wrote what would be called the New Testament. Matthew and Paul began their works in the middle to late 40's AD, and John finished his books no later than the end of the first century. Thus, the New Testament was recorded only 30 or so years after the life of Jesus, which carries great credence to the authenticity of the Gospels and the rest of the New Testament.

## Why Do We Have Both an Old Testament and a New Testament?

The answer to this question becomes clearer when the term 'testament" is defined. The word testament means "covenant" or "promise." When God chose to interact with the Israelites and made them his chosen people, a covenant was established with them. This covenant was established by adherence to the moral, civil, and ceremonial laws of Moses. Historically, the Old Testament era ended with the return from Babylonian and Persian exile around 400 BC. The New Testament is the fulfillment of the Old Testament just as

Jesus is the fulfillment of Judaism (the Law of Moses). As Christians, we are under the New Covenant, meaning that Jesus is our high priest and king (Hebrews 2:17; 3:1). We do not follow the civil and ceremonial laws of Moses, although the timeless moral laws (the Ten Commandments) are required of us considering they are the reflection of God's very nature (Matthew 5:17–20). Although there is a distinction between the Old and New Testaments, we should not make the error of assuming the Old Testament is not important. Paul told Timothy in his final letter that all Scripture is from God and profitable for instruction (2 Timothy 3:16).

## How Do We Know the Bible Is True When Compared With Other Writings?

There are many different avenues to take in order to answer this question, but to keep this brief I will focus on three main points: the historical and literary accuracy of the Bible, the resurrection of Jesus Christ, and the affirmation of the Holy Spirit. As we unpack these, I urge you to research these various claims yourself. You should also become familiar with the term **Christian Apologetics.** The word *apologetics* simply means, "to give a defense" (1 Peter 3:15). Believers should always be ready to defend their faith from attacks in a wise and winsome manner. Studying apologetics is a marvelous endeavor to strengthen one's faith.

First off, the Bible has never been proven inaccurate when it comes to historical claims. Its teachings on persons, events, and places in history have been proven true by archeology and other hard sciences time and again. In regards to literature, unlike other ancient documents, the Bible passes the tests of literary criticism.

The New Testament began to be composed no more than 20 years after the death of Christ with thousands of copies in circulation. When compared to the few copies and the hundreds of years between other ancient documents and the events that inspired them, the Bible stands up to the test. As for the Old Testament, countless scribes composed and recopied the original material with meticulous accuracy and attention to detail, thus the accuracy of the copies from the source material seems trustworthy.

According to the apostle Paul, the trustworthiness of the Christian faith rests on a single event: the literal, bodily resurrection of Jesus Christ. Writing to the church in Corinth, Paul asserts that if Christ did not rise from the dead the Christian faith is practiced in vain, Christians should be pitied, and believers in Christ have no hope for the future (1 Corinthians 15:12–19). Paul continues however by asserting that Christ did rise from the dead, appearing to over 500 hundred people (1 Corinthians 15:3–8). Paul affirmed the resurrection of Christ as a historical event promised from long ago that was affirmed by the writers of the Gospels. Note that according to the New Testament, Christ rose from the dead in a literal body. He was not a ghost; he ate, drank, and could be touched by the disciples (Luke 24:30; John 20:26–27, 21:10–14). History points toward a bodily resurrection of Christ as well as alternate explanations are problematic and inconclusive. For example, some theorize that Jesus never died, but rather fainted on the cross and left the tomb once he regained consciousness. This is problematic on three levels: Romans were efficient executioners that faced punishment if the task was not complete, Jesus could not have moved a large stone and walked past Roman guards, and the disciples recognized Jesus as a man not disfigured and scarred by the lashings. Other alternatives have been offered in order to discredit the New Testament's claim that Christ rose from the dead. However, these claims hold no true credit in academic circles.

Finally, the Holy Spirit himself is evidence in the life of the believer that authenticates true conversion to Christ and the claims of the Bible. According to Jesus, the roles of the Holy Spirit include pointing people to him and revealing his truths (John 14:26, 15:26). The Holy Spirit is evidence that people belong to Christ as the Spirit indwells believers the moment of their conversion (Acts 10:44–45, 11:15–16) and serves as an encourager (Acts 9:31). For the believer, the Holy Spirit resides within providing comfort, encouragement, and insight into the truths of Scripture (Romans 9:1; 2 Corinthians 6:6; Ephesians 3:5; 1 Thessalonians 1:5; Hebrews 10:15–16).

## What Does the Bible Tell Us About the End Times?

It is no surprise that this question would arise considering that we as humans are anxious about our own future. Within the Christian context, believers are ever so curious concerning the last days. Numerous books and articles have been written on the subject of **eschatology** (or "study of the last days"), especially in light of the chaotic world events of the twentieth century and the turn of the millennium. The more one researches this issue, the more questions and differing opinions will arise. Different views concerning the nature of the Rapture, the Antichrist, the Tribulation, and the Millennium are abundant in Christian circles. These different views should not come as a surprise considering the difficult task of interpreting the book of Revelation. The Bible is unclear on many of the details concerning the end of time and Jesus plainly told his followers that it was not for them "to know the times or seasons" in Acts 1:7. Thus, there are some aspects to the last days that we as humans will not know until the events unfold. In the meantime we are to be about bringing people into God's kingdom, preparing them for the last days (Matthew 28:18–20; Acts 1:8).

However, the events of the last days are not completely shrouded. The Bible makes it clear that Jesus will return to Earth at some point in the future (Acts 1:11; 3:19–21) not as a suffering servant, but as a righteous king and judge (Philippians 2:5–11; 2 Timothy 4:1; 2 Peter 4:5). Christians are to look forward to this day (John 14:1–4, Colossians 3:4, 2 Thessalonians 1:7, Hebrews 10:25) as we will share in the rewards of the fulfillment and restoration of all things in a new heavens and new earth (John 14:1–4; Revelation 20: 1–8). However for those who do not know Jesus, his second coming will bring judgment and condemnation. The result is eternal separation from God in a literal place called Hell, the ultimate consequence for sin (Revelation 20:11–15). In short, no matter which view one holds in regards to eschatology, there are three truths in regards to the end of days we must comprehend and are non-negotiable. First, Jesus is coming again and will do so quickly and without warning. Secondly, he will come to rule and to judge. Lastly, we need to be ready for his coming again and evangelize to the ends of the earth in order to prepare humanity for Jesus's return and judgment.

# CHAPTER 4

# CHRISTIAN ETHICS

**Is it Against Our Religious Beliefs to Marry Someone of a Different Race?**

The answer to this question is a resounding "No." Nowhere in the Bible will one find prohibitions against marrying a person of a different race. People who argue otherwise do so erroneously by taking verses out of context found in Deuteronomy 7. In this passage, God instructs the nation of Israel not to marry foreigners or outsiders. However, the reason for this was not a racial one. Rather, this prohibition was given for religious purposes. "For they will turn your sons away from following Me to serve other gods; then the anger of the LORD will be kindled against you and He will quickly destroy you. (Deuteronomy. 7:4)." Careful observation of this passage shows us that God desired for his people to stay faithful to him and not serve the idols of the foreigners. Ezra and Nehemiah, hundreds of years after the events of Deuteronomy, warn of the consequences of interreligious marriage. In this context Nehemiah, Ezra, and other leaders have brought back God's people from exile in Persia and are in the process of establishing the nation once again.

During this process, Nehemiah discovered people were ignorant of God's law due to generations of interreligious marriages.

Careful observation of these passages place personal emphasis on holiness and proper worship of God and not skin color (Ezra 9:12; Nehemiah 10:30). The apostle Paul continues this theme by instructing the Corinthian believers to keep their bodies pure (1 Corinthians 6:18–20) by not being in relationship with unbelievers (2 Corinthians 6:14–15). According to Paul, if one belongs to Christ, their body is not their own but Christ's and therefore the believer must not marry an unbeliever. If the Christian marries an unbeliever, they will suffer the same fate as the Israelites who married the idol-worshipping pagans. In other words, the believer will resemble the world more often than the unbeliever will be won to Christ. Christians should see things differently than unbelievers and therefore no cohesion can be possible. Thus, the case is clear that the Christian is free to marry any person (of the opposite gender) from any nationality or ethnic group as long as both parties are followers of Jesus Christ.

Although interracial marriage is not immoral, interracial marriages bring about a unique set of challenges. Cultural norms and societal issues must be taken into consideration. It is hard enough for couples marrying within their culture to introduce one another to new families and ways of life. The challenges are compounded when marrying outside of an ethnic group. Also, just because God may view your marriage favorably doesn't mean your society will do the same. Due to the effects of human sin, blind racial prejudices are rampant in virtually every culture worldwide. While this extremely depressing, it is a reality that can only be remedied by the love of Jesus Christ, in whom there is no distinction.

# What Exactly Does "Sexual Immorality" Mean?

To answer this question study of the original language and their translations will prove helpful. The phrase "sexual immorality" appears 23 times in the NIV translation of the Bible, once in the Old Testament (Numbers 25:1) and 22 times in the New Testament. In the Old Testament, "sexual immorality" is translated from the Hebrew word *liznowt,* which literally means, "to play." In this text from Numbers 25:1, the men of Israel were engaging in immoral sex with the women of Moab. Thus, the men and women were literally "playing the harlot," or "whoring themselves out." The phrase "playing the harlot" was commonly used by God to describe unfaithful Israel when they worshipped idols, comparing them to an unfaithful spouse committing adultery (Ezekiel 16:41; Hosea 4:15). In the New Testament Jesus, Paul, Jude, and John use the phrase "sexual immorality." The Greek word used in these 22 instances is *porneia.* This word is most often translated "fornication," but could be used to imply "unchastity" or "prostitution." The KJV translates *porneia* as "fornication" which includes pre-marital or extra-marital sex.

Both the NIV and the KJV translate these terms correctly. Therefore we can conclude that "sexual immorality" includes sex before marriage and sex outside of marriage (adultery, which is forbidden in the Ten Commandments). God's standards for sex are clear: no sex outside of marriage (Genesis 2:18-24). Furthermore, the bluntest command concerning sexual immorality comes from Paul in 1 Corinthians 6:18: "Flee sexual immorality. All other sins a person commits is outside the body, but whoever sins sexually, sins against their own body." Paul is clear that sexual immorality is a particularly dangerous sin considering that it is against the body, which is a gift and blessing from God and for believers houses the Holy Spirit.

To be sexually immoral, however, includes more than just the acts of fornication (sex before marriage) and adultery. In the Sermon on the Mount, Jesus plainly stated that adultery can take place without the physical act of intercourse (Matthew 5:27-28). Therefore, sexual immorality can be defined any derivation from God's standards for marriage and sex.

## Why is Sex Before Marriage Wrong?

In order to answer this, we must understand that sex is not bad in and of itself. Our society has so perverted, misused, and confused biblical sexual ethics that our minds our wired to think that sex is dirty or unholy. While it is true that the world has perverted the concept of sex, sexual intercourse is a wonderful gift intended for spouses that originated within the mind of God. In other words, God invented sex. He chose this method for humans to continue the human race. However, we must not merely view sex as a physical act intended only for procreation. In God's design, sex is emotional, should never be exploited for selfish gain, and is exclusive. No one else should partake in this activity except a husband and a wife. Genesis 2:24 states that when a man and a woman leave their parents and are joined with a spouse (marriage), they become "one flesh." The Hebrew phrase "one flesh" describes sexual intimacy. The order in which the author of Genesis presents this material is not accidental or random: **marriage comes before sex.** Paul clearly understood this as he wrote to the church at Corinth: "But since sexual immorality is occurring, each man should have sexual relations with his own wife, and each woman with her own husband (1 Corinthians 7:2)." If Paul is urging husbands and wives only to have sex with one another, the immoral behavior to which Paul is referring must be any sexual activity outside of marriage. The authors of the Bible clearly understood that sex outside of marriage was outside of God's standards and therefore sinful. Marriage vows are a covenant and only in a marriage can sex ever be justified. The vows taken before God and the world are the foundation of the relationship, not feelings or sex. Now let us look at some of the reasons people choose to engage in sexual activity before marriage.

When sexual activity happens outside of a marriage relationship, sex is often used to achieve something sex was never meant to, especially without the boundaries of marriage. Sexual relations outside of marriage can never be a selfless act, but there is more to it than just the act itself. What justification is there for sex outside of marriage except emotions and feelings? Yes, sexual intercourse is an emotional act. However, emotions can change with the wind and therefore they alone should not justify engaging in sexual activity. Furthermore, a dating relationship does not have to be justified by sex. Contrary to television sitcoms and romantic movies, a couple can have a perfectly normal, healthy dating relationship without sexual activity. The problem with these couples engaging in sex early (or at all) in the relationship is that sex becomes the basis of the relationship. What happens when the "romantic feelings" have left? Thus, sex is just a means to an end for teenagers. Teenage boys use sex to satisfy urges they have, and most often do not care when, how, or from whom they get sexual activity just as long as it happens. Under these circumstances, sex cannot be holy or selfless, as women become objects for consumption that can be cast aside when feelings wear off or when someone new comes along. On the other hand, teenage girls give up the use of their bodies for sex hoping to receive emotional security. However, it is not uncommon to find that sexual intimacy cannot provide the security they desire so desperately. In fact, for teenage girls increased sexual activity often leads to increased emotional insecurity, as they feel more objectified with each sexual encounter. In short, sex was never designed to bring pleasure alone or emotional security alone. Pure sexual satisfaction can only be reached in a marriage relationship where sex is used not to chase pleasure or feelings, but rather to serve a spouse in the manner God intended.

## If Someone Commits Suicide, Does That Person Automatically Go to Hell?

**No.** The idea that the act of suicide automatically condemns someone to Hell is a popular belief in many churches today. It is not uncommon to find churchgoers that hold this view in many if not all major Christian denominations across the globe. However, while this view may be popular in some circles, it is totally incorrect. Finding the answer to this question is quite a task considering that there is not a verse in Scripture that clearly and definitively answers this question outright. Instead of just relying on one verse to refute this claim, one has to correctly understand the doctrine of salvation in order to find clarity on this issue.

How is a person saved: by faith or works? The obvious answer is by faith. Paul wrote in Ephesians 2:8 we are saved by faith, not works, unless we should brag and claim we could do it on our own. Not convinced yet? I urge you to read Galatians, as the issue of faith and works is the main theme of the book. Thus, people are not saved by things they do, but rather through faith in God and what he did. Now, if people are not saved by works (good deeds in order to earn God's favor) how can people lose their salvation by works? If salvation cannot be gained by good works, how can it be undone by our evil works? The larger issue at hand here is what is called "eternal security of the believer." While many Christians today believe salvation can be lost by their bad deeds, the Bible teaches contrary. John 10:27–29 and Romans 8:31–39 are both passages that attest to the doctrine of "once saved, always saved." Allow me to be clear: people calling themselves Christians that live a lifestyle of unconfessed and unrepentant sin cannot hold to the "once saved, always saved" doctrine as an excuse for their behavior. While a person is not saved by works, obedience is a natural byproduct of a relationship with God. For the person who continually lives an ungodly lifestyle while claiming Christ, eternal security is not the issue. That person must ask if he/she ever came to salvation in the first place.

Getting back the to the suicide issue, many people who believe suicide sends people to Hell and believe Christians can lose their salvation hold this view because of the issue of confessing sins. These people believe that when a Christian sins, they need to be saved again. There are two problems here. First off, no one that claims this view can be certain exactly how much sin causes one lose their salvation. Some say every time you sin you must be saved again, while others claim salvation is again necessary after a lengthy struggle with sin that could've lasted anywhere from a few hours to several years. The problem is there is no way to measure how much sin requires a need for getting saved again. Secondly, 1 Peter 3:18 reads as follows: "For Christ also died for sins once for all, the just for the unjust, so that He might bring us to God, having been put to death in the flesh, but made alive in the spirit." Therefore, Christ died once for all... period and end of discussion. Christians cannot undo their salvation under any circumstance. Do we even realize the sheer audacity it takes for one to believe he or she can undo something God has done? If this were possible, Christ would have to repeat his work on the cross. Herein exists the major flaw with this line of thought: that Christ's work on the cross is insufficient to save to the uttermost. Some people believe suicide sends people to Hell because it does not allow for confession. If someone commits suicide, they obviously cannot confess that sin. This is another grave error. Christ forgave our sins on the cross. Therefore, when we confess sins to him it is not for forgiveness but for confession, acknowledging and turning away from sin in repentance. Christ has already forgiven that sin.

While it is unfortunate that Christians suffer depression to the degree they feel the need to take their own life, it does not condemn them to an eternity separated from God. Only by ignoring God and his standards for mankind completely do people find themselves condemned (John 3:18).

## Is it Possible to be Both Gay and a Christian?

I am not sure this is the right question to ask. The real question at hand here is, "Can I be a Christian while simultaneously living in sin and rebellion from God's moral standards?" The Bible tells us this is not possible (Matthew 7:13–24; 1 John 3:7–10). Since the issue of homosexuality within Christianity is a popular current debate, let's unpack this issue.

When someone asserts one can be both gay and a Christian, there are two things to keep in mind. First off, true biblical Christianity and the homosexual lifestyle are **mutually exclusive.** This means that these two concepts are at odds with one another and cannot coexist. For a person to affirm their homosexuality and their Christianity is completely absurd given the claims of the Bible and the nature of the homosexual lifestyle. To illustrate, a red crayon cannot be both a red crayon and a blue crayon at the same time. The characteristics that make up the color red are in stark contrast from those that make up the blue color. Sure, the two colors can be mixed together, but when this happens the two colors cease to exist. God's standards for marriage and human sexual relations were always intended to be enjoyed between one man and one woman. God ordained marriage (Genesis 2:18-24), and biblical writers such as Paul condemned homosexual behavior (Romans 1:26-27). On the other hand, a person living the homosexual lifestyle completely ignores the standards God has set for sexual behavior. Paul and Peter wrote that Christians are to be slaves of Christ (Romans 6; 1 Peter 2:16) and his righteousness. Slaves do not get to choose which laws to obey. Christ went to the cross to pay for all of the sins of man, holding nothing back from us. Therefore we must obey God in all things, including sexual standards. God's law revealed in the Bible must govern 100% of your life, not 99% (James 2:10).

Secondly, I would like to point out that to be tempted to sin is not the same as sinning. Satan tempted Jesus and the book of James tells us what to do when we are tempted (James 1:13-15; 4:4-8). It is obvious that some people are attracted to people of the same gender thus tempted towards homosexual activity. However, like all temptation it can be combated. It is possible for the Christian to be tempted in any way due to the fallen nature of man (Jeremiah 17:9; Romans 3:23) including temptation towards homosexual activity. The difference between the godly individual is that when tempted that person desperately attempts to flee from sin. Christians are not immune to sin and sometimes indulge in sinful behavior. The Christian, when this happens, will confess and repent from their sin and attempt to better live a life of holiness and righteousness (1 John 1:9–2:2).

In summary, it is very unlikely someone actively and without abandon pursuing a lifestyle characterized by homosexual behavior can be a redeemed follower of Christ. It is impossible to be a Christ follower while totally disregarding his standards towards sexual conduct. On the other hand, it is possible to be a Christian tempted towards homosexuality, recognizing that homosexuality is a sin against God, and doing their utmost to avoid sinful behavior. The sin of homosexuality is no different from any other sin in that the temptation must be fought, actions must be confessed, and repentance must take place.

## Some People Say Jesus Never Taught on Homosexuality. Is This True?

Proponents of the homosexual agenda, especially those simultaneously claiming homosexuality and Christianity, are quick to argue that Jesus did not condemn homosexuality. This argument not only fails logically, but also is incongruent and incompatible with the entirety of the Scripture. It is true that Jesus never explicitly addressed the issue of homosexuality outright. However, further examination of Jesus's teachings in the Gospels proves it is incorrect to claim that Jesus was silent in regards to God's standards concerning marriage and sexual behavior.

While Jesus never explicitly condemned homosexuality, he did so by default. Never did Jesus teach contrary to Scripture. In fact during his ministry he affirmed the entirety of the Old Testament Law (Matthew 5:17–19). More specifically, Jesus affirmed God's standards for marriage when asked about relationships in eternity. Jesus taught that in the resurrection (what we would refer to as "in Heaven") people would not marry **or be given in marriage** (Matthew 22:30; Mark 12:25; Luke 20:35). Note the distinction between "marriage and given in marriage." In this culture, this distinction would have been understood to denote gender. Those who marry would have been the males, while those who are given to marry would be the females. This is not hard for us to comprehend as this custom is still practiced today in our culture as a bride is given away to the groom in many wedding ceremonies. Jesus further affirmed marriage as between one man and one woman for life when questioned about divorce. Matthew records when asked about marriage and divorce by certain Pharisees, Jesus quoted Genesis 2:24, reinforcing the marriage of one man and one woman (Matthew 19:4–6). Mark also records this event in his Gospel account (Mark 10:5–9). Time and again, Jesus pointed his followers and skeptics alike to the Old Testament to affirm his teachings and reinforce Scripture as the standard for morality, including sexual ethics. It would be impossible for Jesus to condone homosexuality given his devotion and reliance to the teachings of the Old Testament.

Some wonder why Jesus did not take the time to specifically condemn homosexuality in his ministry. The answer to this question is defined in one word: **audience.** Jesus primarily ministered in Jewish communities in Palestine. In first century

41

Palestine, the Jews still followed the Old Testament thoroughly and likely would not have struggled with homosexuality. It is unlikely devout Jewish communities in this time would contain open, practicing homosexuals. Paul, on the other hand, served in Greece and Rome where homosexuality was more common and acceptable. Paul addressed this issue (Romans 1:26–27; 1 Corinthians 6:9–11; 1 Timothy 1:9–10) as problematic to his ministry whereas Jesus likely did not encounter homosexuality in Palestine.

## Seeing That We Are to Look Out For Our Brothers and Sisters in Christ, How Do You Tell Someone They're Sinning and They Need to Stop?

This is one of the hardest aspects of the Christian life for many reasons. Who wants to be the one to have to initiate the awkward conversation? We are scared of losing friends. We are scared of being labeled as holier-than-thou. We may feel inadequate because of the sin in our own lives to start addressing sin in others. Besides, doesn't the Jesus tell us to "take the plank out of your eye before focusing on others", to "judge not, unless you be judged yourself?" Doesn't that exclude us from ever having to call out one of our Christian friends in sin?

Not exactly. While we are not to judge (because Jesus is the only righteous judge) and we have no authority to condemn, that doesn't mean we are forced into silence when we see sin in the life of a Christian friend. Paul in Ephesians 4:25 encourages believers to speak truth with one another because they are called out together. Paul wrote to this church to tell them when one falls into sin it has the potential to affect the entire body of believers. If sin goes on unchecked, the results for the individual and the church could be disastrous. However, it is not just important **that** this takes place but **how** this takes place. You cannot go into a conversation like this with a haughty, proud spirit. Remember there is sin in your life, too. That is why Jesus had the conversation about planks in the eye. Furthermore, consider the words of Paul in Galatians 6:1–2, "Brothers, if anyone is caught in any transgression, you who are spiritual should restore him in a spirit of gentleness. Keep watch on yourself, lest you too be tempted. Bear one another's burden as so fulfill the law of Christ (ESV)." According to Paul, a person who is growing and active in his or her faith should take action to restore someone who is struggling or falling away. This should be done only in a humble and gentle manner. You don't want to come across like the "turn or burn" guys that stand on the street corner with bullhorns and signs screaming condemnation at the masses. Paul also warns in this verse to keep some focus on yourself that you are not tempted. The temptation here could be twofold: we could either be tempted into pride by thinking that we are right and therefore better than the person falling into sin or we could be tempted into the sin that the person struggled with in the first place. Finally, Paul claims by doing this we fulfill the law of Christ. Jesus cares about his church; he loved His church so much that he did not want to see it fall into sin and be corrupted or destroyed. If sin is allowed to go unchecked or without question, the church will fail to be the church and will look too much like the world. The early church leaders knew this and therefore issued multiple challenges for holding one another accountable (Romans 15:1–7; 1 Corinthians 6.1–8; Colossians 3:16; 1Thessalonains 5:11; James 5:16–20).

Some good practical advice is to do this within your own circle of friends. A wise word from a friend is most helpful and true friends may not like it at first, but will be thankful in the long run. Also hold yourself to the same standard you hold others. If they feel that they can be honest with you when you mess up (and you will mess up!), the honesty and accountability is more likely to be reciprocated when you need to address an issue with them. Always keep a calm and humble sprit; try not to get angry or defensive when challenged. The goal of these conversations should be repentance and restoration, not judgment, condemnation, and isolation. We would all be wise to remember the words of Paul in 1 Corinthians 13:1–3, "If I speak in the tongues of men or of angels, but do not have love, I am only a resounding gong or a clanging cymbal. If I have the gift of prophecy and can fathom all mysteries and all knowledge, and if I have a faith that can move mountains, but do not have love, I am nothing. If I give all I possess to the poor and give over my body to hardship that I may boast, but do not have love, I gain nothing." Love for our fellow Christian has to be seen in these conversations. If you don't genuinely love the person that you have to talk to, don't even bother. There is a huge plank in your eye.

## What if You Have a Conversation With Someone About Their Sin and They Get Mad at You and Refuse to Stop?

Due to the nature of human emotions these conversations can be extremely awkward and troublesome. Regardless of your approach, a negative outcome may be inevitable. Although this may be the case it shouldn't deter us from doing what is right. If the person responds negatively, there are some things we can do. First, understand that it is not us who changes people. Don't try to do God's job. Just spread his love and his message and let the Holy Spirit do the convicting. Secondly, control how you react. I have always tried to reiterate with students in my ministry that they cannot control others, only themselves. If a Christian brother/sister gets defensive over an issue in which they are acting contrary to God's word they are likely under extreme denial or conviction. Don't get drawn into a heated argument where you will lose your testimony; that's not what God wants. Finally, never forget to keep praying for them. Paul tells us in 1 Thessalonians to pray without ceasing. That is the attitude you must take. Sometimes the best thing to do when a situation like that turns negative is to stop talking to them and start praying. Pray for wisdom on how to interact with that person. Pray for patience. Pray that person repents and asks God for forgiveness. Pray for yourself, that you be kept humble and aware of your own shortcomings during this process. Following these three steps I believe is good, biblical advice but may not always solve the problem. Situations and the people within them are unpredictable. Things may not always have a good ending. However, we are called to do what is right in all situations so that God may get the glory (Matthew 5:13–16).

Jesus offered practical advice on this issue that serves as model for church discipline. Sadly, many churches practice church discipline infrequently, if at all. In Matthew 18: 15–17, Jesus taught when someone is doing something sinful or unwise, one person should go that person and address it. If the person does not take that well or refuses to repent, then two or three people should go as witnesses so the issue can be addressed again. If the issue is not resolved during the first two steps, the issue should be brought before the church. If the person is still unrepentant and refuses to stop doing something that is potentially damaging to the church, the person should be asked to leave the church and should not be treated as a brother or sister in Christ until such a time that they repent. If the person repents, fellowship should be restored and they should be welcomed back. Again, as with personal relationships, the ultimate goal is repentance and restoration. We don't do these things so we can feel holier-than-thou and get full of pride because of our own righteousness. Remember, our own righteousness is like filthy rags before God's holiness (Isaiah 64:6).

Although the words of Jesus are true and wise, it is rare that a situation ever gets to the third step of bringing a particular sin before the church. In an ideal setting, sins are confessed personally and amongst close friends so there is no need to take unrepentant sin before the church. I have been in church my whole life and have only seen this happen once. Just because this rarely happens, it doesn't mean churches shouldn't do this if necessary. Christ loves his church, which is why he is so adamant about keeping it healthy and holy. Sin is like cancer. If detected and treated early things may work out. If not, the consequences could get really nasty.

## How Do You Respond to Someone Who Verbally Attacks and Disrespects Your Beliefs?

Jesus said a servant is no greater than the master (John 15:20). This means that if the master is harassed, the servants are not exempt from harassment either. Christians have been persecuted from the onset of the church. Why? Jesus himself was oftentimes met with doubt, persecution, and rejection when sharing his message, the same message we share today (hopefully we do)! It doesn't take long to scan the Gospels to find one of many of his confrontations with the religious establishment of the day (Matthew 3:7,12:24; Mark

2:16; Luke 14:3; John 8). At one point, his own family thought he was losing it and came to take him home (Mark 3:21-31). During his trial, the Sanhedrin mocked him (Matthew 26:57-67), Herod thought he was crazy (Luke 23), the soldiers that took him to the cross made fun of him (Matthew 27:27) and one of the thieves hurled insults to Jesus as they were dying (Matthew 27:38-44). Let's not forget that Judas, one of Jesus' best friends, betrayed him, Peter denied ever knowing him, and his closest friends fled when he was arrested (John 18). So essentially, if you want to follow Jesus you will be following someone who was constantly harassed and insulted, abandoned by his friends, and was betrayed by one of his best friends and murdered.

So the question is how we respond like Jesus when we are challenged for our beliefs. For us some practical advice would be to first off make sure we are right according to Scripture. Jesus responded with Scripture when tempted (Matthew 4) and never deviated from biblical truth when challenged. Make sure that you views are aligned with the Bible. Secondly, don't get drawn into a defensive, heated, debate where tempers get flared and the goal is to win an argument. Remember Paul's words in 1 Corinthians 13? If you don't have love for others, what you're saying really doesn't matter even if it is true. Finally, remember that Jesus was persecuted so you get to share in his sufferings as a disciple that comes with rewards not only here but in the hereafter. Consider the words of Jesus in the Sermon on the Mount: "Blessed are you when people insult you, persecute you and falsely say all kinds of evil against you because of me. Rejoice and be glad, because great is your reward in heaven, for in the same way they persecuted the prophets who were before you. (Matthew 5:11-12)." Jesus knew his disciples would be insulted and face persecution which is why he told the disciples to be as wise a serpents, but harmless as doves (Matthew 10:16). Know persecution will come if you follow Jesus. Know how to handle it.

## Does Jesus Get Angry When We re Disrespectful to Our Parents?

All sin angers and hurts the heart of God. Sin is a big deal; sin put Jesus on the cross ... **your sin!** Do not ever undermine and downplay the gravity of sin. Sin is any attitude or action contrary to God's standards for our lives. Remember the penalty for sin is death; the spiritual death and eternal separation from God to a sinner's Hell (Romans 6:23). Furthermore, the Bible tells us that God is holy, cannot let sin go unpunished forever, takes no delight in the actions of sinful people, and that our sin puts us at enmity with God (Psalms 5:4; Isaiah 6:3; Romans 9:14; Revelation 6:8).

Obviously, God does not hide his feelings towards sin, nor does he mix words by making a command to honor parents in the Ten Commandments found in Exodus 20. The fifth commandment is to honor parents that one's days would be long upon the earth. This is the only commandment with a promise! Obey your parents, honor your parents and your life will be blessed and you will more than likely live longer due to accepting their wisdom and guidance. Now this isn't an absolute, considering that young people who follow this command can and do die. However, the premise holds true: you're more than likely to have a blessed life when you submit to the authority of your parents. Nor is this an absolute in the case of some parents who abuse their children. If parents are putting children in a situation that is harmful to the child, things get a little messy. While I would advise children to continue to love and respect their parents, obeying them in some circumstances may not be the best course of action. These extreme examples are few and far between, although I have encountered them in my ministry.

However, as youth pastor 99.99% of my discussions on this issue concern students who need to respect and honor the authority of their parents. If a student desires to maintain an effective Christian witness and wants to be a leader in my youth ministry, respecting parents is foundational and critical. If a student wants to be a leader in my youth ministry, I better notice them respecting their parents on a consistent basis. The way Christian teenagers address their parents speaks volumes to their spiritual maturity.

## What Does the Bible Say About Stress?

Have you ever heard the phrase, "I'm too blessed to be stressed?" Yeah, I have, too. It stresses me out. I am not sure of the origins of the phrase but I can tell you it cannot be found in the Bible. Furthermore, does the line of reasoning behind that phrase really hold water? Where in the Bible are we ever promised that we will be exempt from the stress of life? Scripture does speak to the blessings of living an obedient life (Psalms and Proverbs) and certainly avoiding sin and its consequences is less stressful. But what about the days with the flat tire? What about the toddler who never stops running, screaming, and bangs your pots and pans on the kitchen floor so loudly you think your ears will bleed? For the teen, do you ever feel so blessed that you never stress about grades, college applications, getting a cool car, or trying to manage that pesky acne? It seems that even for the devoted, obedient Christian stress is an unavoidable part of the human experience. I can relate to stress. As

I was writing this entry my 22-month old son split his eyebrow open on a marble windowsill. Driving 45 minutes in traffic to the hospital with his mom (whose nerves were shot) and an injured toddler that ended up with three stitches will cause one to stress! But again, what does the Bible say about dealing with these situations?

We shouldn't be discouraged that we will never be exempt from stress. We should delight in the fact that God promises us his presence during those times. A quick look at Scripture shows us many people devoted to the Lord experienced times of great stress. Imagine how Abraham felt marching up the mountainside with his son, Isaac, not knowing if they were both going to make the trip back down. Put yourself in Moses's shoes if you can: a stuttering murderer tasked with leading an entire nation of people out of slavery. Let us not forget Elijah fled for his life after the Mount Carmel experience when an evil queen named Jezebel tried to have him killed. No one would deny that these three heroes of the Old Testament walked closely with God and experienced the blessings of obedience. Nowhere in the lives of these men did God ever promise they would not experience difficulty. In fact, the more they obeyed God the more likely they would encounter stress. Try to imagine the look on these men's faces if someone were to come up to them and tell them they were "too blessed to be stressed." So what are we to do with this? Look at the promises of God in the midst of their trials. Abraham was promised a lamb, which served as a foreshadowing of Christ and a picture of the Gospel. Moses was told that I AM would be at his side when Pharaoh asked who demanded the Israelites be let go. Elijah was promised provision and renewal of his strength to continue his ministry. It was God who sustained them in the midst of their stress and his presence was enough for these men to be obedient and persevere.

Don't forget that Jesus was stressed, too. The Son of God, the creator of the universe experienced so much stress the night before his crucifixion that the blood vessels popped in his face and blood mixed with his sweat. Jesus was blessed. He was also stressed. Paul experienced almost every kind of stress in ministry including beatings, insults, betrayal, and even a shipwreck (2 Corinthians 11). Paul certainly was no stranger to stress. Again, both Jesus and Paul relied on the presence of God during their time of suffering.

I leave you with a verse that has helped me when I am afflicted by the stress of life. Paul, writing from imprisonment, encouraged believers to trust in God:

"Be anxious for nothing, but in every situation by prayer and petition make your requests known to God. And the peace which transcends all understating will guard your hearts and minds in Christ Jesus (Philippians 4:6–7)."

## What Does it Mean to Covet?

The tenth commandment tells us not to covet things that belong to our neighbor (Exodus 20:17; Deuteronomy 5:21). The word "covet" means to want something inappropriately with no regard to the owner or the object. To simply desire something is not a bad thing. One could desire a job, a wife, a new computer, or a cheeseburger. In many Eastern worldviews, to have desire is negative all the time and these views teach that desire leads to suffering. The Bible does not teach this. What the Bible does teach, especially in the tenth commandment, is that misplaced and inappropriate desire is sinful and will lead to other sin. Coveting is present and is at the root of all sin. Sinful actions are the results

51

of a selfish heart. Coveting involves wanting things that don't belong to you or things you didn't earn. Coveting often involves products, riches, spouses, or jobs. You can also covet things that are not tangible, such as talent, success, influence, or relationships. It is also important to note that coveting is a twofold sin. Coveting begins with not being content in what God has given you. Coveting then evolves from simply not being content to finding ways to obtain things. James asserts that sin begins with desire, which leads to action (James 1:13–15).

## Are Those in the Military That Have to Kill Others in Combat Guilty of Murder?

Although there are other Christians who may disagree with me on this issue, I would say those engaged in combat are not guilty of breaking the sixth commandment. When one examines the sixth commandment, "Thou shall not kill," and places a prohibition of the taking of any human life under any circumstance, they do so at the peril of not taking into account the rest of Scripture. Furthermore, I believe the effect this verse should have on us is to respect life, more specifically innocent life. I am a proponent of capital punishment (although not as excitedly as some would like) considering that after the flood in Genesis 9 God commanded that whoever took life that their life should be required. God does not do this because he is not compassionate (he spared Cain after Abel's murder and allowed David to live after the death of Uriah). Conisdering humans are made in the image of God, murder is an attack on his character and therefore must be punished severely. I know the question was about warfare but you must understand that not all killing is forbidden by the Ten Commandments.

In Scripture war is presented as a reality in a lost, fallen, and sinful world. Many detractors of the Bible point to the conquest of Canaan seen in the Old Testament and paint God as war-mongerer. That fails to paint an accurate picture of God who used his people to combat wicked nations that had oppressed others after God had given them centuries to repent. Seeing that God did command the conquest of Canaan (Joshua 5:14, 8:1–2) and oversaw battle for Saul (1 Samuel 15) and David (2 Samuel 5) it would be impossible to say that all war is inherently sinful. That's not to say that war is never bad; war is a terrible thing. However, sometimes it is necessary to achieve a morally acceptable goal. In the New Testament, neither Jesus nor the early church members ever prohibited Christians from military service, even when interacting with soldiers (Luke 3:14; Matthew 8, Acts 10). In fact, Paul uses military analogies when discussing spiritual matters (1 Corinthians 9:7; 2 Corinthians 10:4; Ephesians 6; 2 Timothy 2:3).

To summarize, the New Testament writers had ample opportunity to condemn and prohibit military combat for Christians but did not. Therefore we are left with our own conscience to decide whether one should serve in military combat. While it may not be sinful, it may not be beneficial to do so either under a variety of circumstances given the violent nature of combat and the new studies done on PTSD (Post-Traumatic Stress Disorder). The price of freedom is always costly and there will always be a need for combat in this sinful world. It is up for the Christian to decide if military combat is for them or not.

# Is it a Sin For a Christian to Drink Alcohol?

This is a complicated question that requires more than a simple "yes" or "no." In order to get to the heart of this issue believers must ask themselves two questions. First, is it sinful to drink alcohol? Secondly, is it beneficial to drink alcohol? The Bible clearly teaches that to be drunk is a sin, as this causes believers not to be of their right mind, making them more prone to sinful actions and impairing their ability to maintain a Christian witness (Ephesians 5:18). However, I will be perfectly clear to impart to you what the Bible *does and does not say* about the consumption of alcohol without being drunk which is more commonly referred to as casual or social drinking. The Bible does not teach that drinking is a sinful act in and of itself (Psalm 104:14, Ecclesiaties 9:7). However, Paul does warn in 1 Corinthians 6:12–13 that while some actions may not necessarily be considered sinful, they may not be beneficial for the life of the believer. Given our culture's bent toward alcoholism, its abuses, and its devastating effects on our culture, it is hard to envision a scenario where drinking does not harm the testimony of the believer. For a Christian to participate in the consumption of alcohol with a flippant, cavalier attitude with total disregard to the consequences is a grave error. Furthermore, Paul also warns in the aforementioned verses that some actions that may be lawful, but not beneficial and may be a stumbling block for others.

Paul discusses this issue further in Romans 14 and 1 Corinthians 8. In these passages, believers were torn over the issue of eating meat that had been offered up to idols in temple worship. Some Christians saw this as a problem whereas others did not. Paul warns to those who did partake of this meat to be careful so they would not cause others to stumble in their faith and cause division within the body of Christ. In light of Paul's instruction here, if a believer does not have an issue with the consumption of alcohol but his brother or sister in Christ does, the believer needs to be aware that their consumption of alcohol could cause problems for others. Even if you drink and do not abuse alcohol whatsoever, a younger, less mature Christian who looks to you as an example may be led into sin. Surely, a believer would not want to cause problems for other believers simply because they could not pass on alcohol. Furthermore, if your brothers and sisters in Christ are offended by alcohol, you could be opening up the door for division within the church and hurting the body of Christ. At this point a believer must ask which is more important: a desire to enjoy a beverage or the unity and well being of the body of Christ.

Another interesting point in the discussion is this: if being drunk is a sin, why drink in the first place? Why take unnecessary steps that would take you closer to sinfulness? A Christian should take every effort they can to avoid sin, to stay above reproach, and to flee the very appearance of evil. When people drink they are allowing themselves to be closer to sin than the person who chooses to abstain. People may look at the stance of total abstinence as legalistic and while some who choose to abstain may take a legalistic approach, my approach comes from a concern for the body of Christ, the pursuit of holiness, and not causing others to stumble.

## Are Christians Allowed to Eat Pork?

Now here is a question you may never get asked. This was a new one for me! When a student in my youth ministry discovered there were dietary restrictions in the Old Testament that prevented the consumption of pork, this became the next inevitable and obvious topic. Are Christians allowed to consume pork (or other foods such as crustaceans, shellfish, etc.)? In short, Christians today are not bound to the religious dietary laws given to the nation of Israel during the time of Moses. Therefore, Christians are allowed to eat in freedom Let's unpack the issue.

It is helpful to understand that there were three different types of laws found in the Pentateuch, the first five books of the Bible penned by Moses. There was the **Moral Law** (the Ten Commandments and their applications) that dealt with ethics towards God and other people. These are still in play and are applicable to Christians today. Jesus affirmed these laws constantly in the New Testament, heavily in the Sermon on the Mount, and Paul affirmed the believer should not abandon moral law (Romans 6:15). The second type of laws given were **civil laws**, which applied to theocratic (meaning God ruled nation) Israel which included building codes, property stewardship, financial guidelines, and other miscellaneous cultural issues (Exodus 21:12–36). Finally, **ceremonial laws** were also a component of the Law of Moses. These laws were religious in nature and dealt with proper temple decorum, **dietary restrictions**, animal sacrifices, feasts and festivals, etc. (Leviticus 21; 22:17–31). The Christian today is not bound to the ceremonial and civil law of ancient, theocratic Israel. The ceremonial and civil laws were time bound applications of the moral law. The New Testament teaches emphatically Jesus, our High Priest, is the fulfillment of the Old Testament sacrificial/ temple system (Hebrews 4). Jesus made the ultimate sacrifice, which nullified animal sacrifices, and no temple is needed because the Holy Spirit dwells within the believer (Galatians 5:22–23; Ephesians 5:18).

Finally, back to pork. If ceremonial laws that included dietary restrictions does not bind the Christian, believers can freely consume pork if they so desire. This issue was part of the debate of the Jerusalem council recorded in Acts 15. The argument arose because some of the Jewish converts wanted new Gentile (non-Jewish) Christians to adhere to the Mosaic Law. After much deliberation, the church leaders decided these Gentiles should not be bound to the restrictions of the Jewish laws. In light of all this, I eat pork. I do so most of the time with my church members. On a personal note, I find the pig to be the tastiest creature God put on Earth. However, I am aware that pork, ham, and bacon are not the healthiest of foods. It would be wise to consult a doctor before going "hog-wild" on this issue.

# CHAPTER 5

# THE CHURCH

### Is Church Involvement Really That Important?

I'm sure you have heard someone say something along these lines: "*I believe in God, but I don't go to church because:*

*-I can worship God in my own way*

*-You don't need to go to church to be a good Christian*

*-The church is flawed and full of hypocrites*

*-Church is not relevant anymore*

*-The world is my church, and that's where I serve God"*

Of course you have. If you have been involved in church for a period of time you have undoubtedly heard numerous reasons why people claiming to have a personal relationship with Jesus Christ are not involved in a local community of faith. As a pastor, it frustrates me to no end. I know why lost people do not faithfully attend church:

they are lost people. Real complicated, huh? Although it takes more thought, I have also figured out why people claiming Christ neglect the body of Christ, and the answer is twofold.

First, it is quite possible and very likely that someone claiming Christ while ignoring the commands of Scripture has never been genuinely converted (Matthew 7:21-23). Now don't misunderstand me; I am not proclaiming a works-based system that requires church attendance for salvation. What I am saying is that a true converted Christian should have no qualms about being a part of the body of Christ that seeks to serve the Lord by fulfilling the Great Commission via the local church.

Secondly, the Christians neglecting the local body of faith are actively engaged in willful disobedience. The New Testament model of believers serving God, serving others, and fulfilling the Great Commission is through the vehicle of involvement in a local church. I agree with the pastor who said once of his church's outreach program, " I can't understand why we spend so much of our outreach time begging saved people to come to church."

I will unpack my case by responding to the aforementioned objections to church involvement with my responses matching each objection in sequential order:

-You can worship God, but not in your own way. The Christian faith is not some privatized matter that is open to your personal subjective feelings. The New Testament makes it clear that the church (universally and locally) is God's plan for the world. There is no Plan B, and God is not looking for suggestions from us on how to improve upon Acts 1:8.

-A person redeemed by Christ should have no problem with church involvement. Should you not want to be about serving the one who saved you and making his love and grace known to others? How can you allow others to not know about the wonderful gift of Christ's salvation by neglecting evangelism and discipleship? Besides this and the New Testament model of church polity, the book of Hebrews explicitly calls for believers to gather together (Hebrews 3:12–13; 10:25).

-The church is full of hypocrites and sinners. If you join, there will be one more. The church is flawed because it is full of imperfect people marred by the effects of their sin. However, you are in no position to bash the church on this issue. The church is the bride of Christ, and I don't know of any groom that wants to see his bride mistreated or neglected. Christ died for imperfect people, including you and those within the church you so callously judge. Paul served churches knowing they were full of sinful people that were going to have problems. That's why he penned verses that encouraged the believers to build one another up in the Lord and strengthen the body (Romans 14:19; 1 Corinthians 10:23; Ephesians 4:12–16; 1 Thessalonians 5:11).

-This objection is sometimes accurate, but not entirely. Yes, there are many churches that have difficulty reaching the culture of the 21$^{st}$ century. Many churches cannot or choose not to adopt methods or ideas that would appeal to the current culture. A respected church planter once said, "If the 1950s come back, we're ready." Ouch. However, let me be clear: the Gospel always relevant no matter if the church is contemporary or traditional. How can the Gospel ever be irrelevant? People will always be sinful in need of Jesus. Thankfully, some churches have found ways to present the Gospel in effective ways, both traditional and contemporary. Also, no matter what kind of church, whether an old-fashioned country church or inner city contemporary church plant, if the Gospel is not at the center, it's not a church. In other words, while churches change, the Gospel does not. No matter what methods the churches implement, the Gospel message must never be compromised under any circumstances.

-I would be interested to see the people claiming this lifestyle give the statistics on how many they reach for Christ. Shooting pool in a bar, sitting a tree stand, surfing on the beach, or having coffee at Starbucks is not church. Folks making this claim forget the reason the church gathers. Church isn't about you. It's about worshipping God and serving others. We worship God through song, lifestyle, the preaching of the Word, etc. We serve others by sharing our faith, meeting needs, and discipling others in the faith. So, for those of you who watch a televangelist on Sunday morning in your bathrobe with a bowl of oatmeal and call it "church," you are in grave error. The word "church" in Greek is *ekklesia*, meaning "the called out ones." Also, for those who are wondering, the church is not a building. It's people.

## Why Do People Get Baptized?

Christians are encouraged to be baptized shortly after their placing their faith in Jesus for several reasons. Primarily and most importantly it is out of obedience to the command and example Christ set. In the Great Commission, Jesus commanded his followers to go into the entire world teaching, making disciples, and baptizing (Matthew 28:18–20). Furthermore, Matthew, Mark, and Luke record the baptism of Jesus (John indirectly describes the event) as a significant point in his life and the beginning of his ministry. Jesus' baptism is also seen is an example to believers; Jesus was baptized (although he was sinless) therefore Jesus's followers should be baptized.

Before we go any further, baptism does not save anyone from their sin. There is nothing magical or holy about the water. Salvation comes by repentance in God's grace through the work of Christ on the cross. So why is baptism important? Practically speaking, baptism identifies the believer with Christ in the presence of a local body of believers. Paul tells believers in Galatia that when they are baptized they are "clothed with Jesus" (Galatians 3:27). According to Paul, baptism is an outward expression of the inward work Christ has done in the life of the believer. Baptism (by immersion) also symbolizes the death, burial, and resurrection of Jesus. When I baptize someone, as the person is under the water I will say (very quickly!) something like, "buried with Christ in death." As I bring the person back up I will say, "raised to walk in a new life." My pastor from my childhood used to say "raised in the likeness of his resurrection." The symbolic nature of baptism carries a second meaning, too. Baptism also symbolizes the death of the old person (or our sinful, lost self) and the birth of our new life in Christ. When a person comes to faith in Christ, the old self dies and the new person in Christ is born (2 Corinthians 5:17). The symbolic nature of baptism is significant as it further identifies the new believer with Jesus, showing the witnesses of the baptism that their identity is now with Christ.

*Noah Raulerson*

## Should Women Be Pastors? Why or Why Not?

The pastorate is not designed for women, and vice versa. There is certainly no shortage of debate over this issue, and the debate is often an emotionally heated one. The role of women within the church varies across Christian denominations. Some ordain women into the pastorate, while others do not. Some churches allow women to be a paid staff member, but take the title of "director" (for example, *music director, children's director, etc.*). Given the diversity concerning this issue, a simple answer would be hard to come by. The complexity of this issue is further compounded considering the debate on whether or not the Bible explicitly forbids or approves of women in the pastorate. Before I go any further, know that I am not chauvinist nor do I think women are incapable of any leadership roles. In the secular world, some of my best employers and supervisors were women who led with honesty, intelligence, and effectiveness. I have also been in certain cultural settings (Central America) where male leadership in a local church was absent completely, leaving women to carry on the duties of pastor. Thanks be to God that these women were able to lead! However, these women prayed earnestly that God would raise up male leadership in order to more effectively fulfill duties of the pastor. Therefore in light of cases such as these I will not claim that the practice of women in the pastorate is sinful, but it is not ideal.

The specific gender roles described in the Bible serve as a foundational argument for those claiming women should not be pastors. These roles were assigned in creation and within the marriage of Adam of Eve (Genesis 1:26–28; 2:18–25). Paul elaborates on these gender roles in Ephesians 5 teaching male headship, with the husband and wife submitting to each other in various capacities.

Thus, the Bible teaches **complementarian gender roles,** meaning men and women are created with equal worth in God's image, but have distinct functions. In contrast those who would ordain women pastors would more than likely to hold to **egalitarianism,** which teaches that men and women are created equal without distinct functions, denying differing roles for men and women. Egalitarians commit a huge error in assuming that one's worth and function are one in the same.

It is safe to ascertain Paul carried the idea of complementarian gender roles into church governance and polity. Paul writes to Timothy: "A woman should learn in quietness and full submission. I do not permit a woman to teach or to assume authority over a man, she must be quiet. For Adam was formed first, then Eve. And Adam was not the one deceived; it was the woman who was deceived and became a sinner (2 Timothy. 2:11–14)." Unfortunately, ignorant, chauvinist pastors have twisted this passage, which has led to women being poorly treated and verbally abused in some settings. Paul never meant for women to be fully dominated and controlled by men, never speaking a word during Bible study time, or to even forbid them from leading a small group Bible study. Paul did not want gender roles to be misunderstood and abused in the church. Men should carry out duties associated with pastors/elders, which Paul explicitly states. By reminding Timothy of the story of Adam and Eve, Paul illustrates that the first sin was committed because Adam and Eve did not follow the gender roles God gave them (Genesis 3). By taking part in sin, Eve usurped the role the man in an attempt to lead Adam. Paul is not implying that Eve (and all women) was intellectually inferior to the man, but that Eve willfully attempted to take on the role of the man. Adam was just as guilty considering that he was not looking out for his wife by allowing her to lead him into sin. Instead of fulfilling his role as a servant leader, Adam decided to indulge in prideful sin along with his spouse. In light of this, Paul thought it unwise for women to lead a congregation in the office of the pastorate because it reflected the reversal of gender roles innate within human nature.

This does not mean women are forbidden to serve in their leadership capacities. Since Paul speaks exclusively of the pastorate in the aforementioned passage found in 1 Timothy, women's roles in modern churches can vary. Personally though I prefer male leadership in the pastorate, I would be comfortable with women's leadership in music or children's ministry. Given the nature of teens and the struggles they face, I cannot recommend placing a woman in a pastoral role within a student ministry. It should also be noted that two places in the New Testament (Romans 16:1–2; 1 Timothy 3:11) women appear as deacons, although some argue the latter passage refers to wives of deacons. In Romans 16: 1–2, Paul mentions Phoebe by name, a deaconess that faithfully assisted Paul and the church. Women in many churches today benefit from a strong women's ministry coordinator. While women should not fill the role of the pastor/shepherd, women should seek to use their time, talents, and treasures to serve God, serve the church, and fulfill the Great Commission.

## Should Women Be Allowed to Speak in Church in Reference to 1 Corinthians 14:34?

*(Before reading this answer, it would behoove you to refer to the previous question concerning women in the pastorate. Although the questions are*

*different, the view of biblical gender roles is explained and terms used in this answer are defined in the aforementioned section.)*

This is a loaded, controversial topic that I can by no means give a full comprehensive or universally appeasing response. Nevertheless, this verse was written under the inspiration of the Holy Spirit and because of Paul's concern for the health of the church at Corinth it requires our attention. The verse in question is 1 Corinthians 14:34, "Women should remain silent in the churches. They are not allowed to speak, but must be in submission as the law says." Many people today see this verse as misogynistic and reject the verse altogether in disgust. On the other hand, some folks have even gone so far as to use this verse to promote and practice this verse legalistically in their churches, forbidding women of any public speaking or teaching. Neither view seems logical or correct given the context of 1 Corinthians 14. In this chapter, Paul urges the Corinthians to practice good order in their worship services because God is a God of order, not disorder and confusion (14:33). Paul gave specific instructions concerning hymns, tongues, and doctrine while stating that all should be done to build up the body (14:26). Therefore, when Paul addresses the issue of women teaching he does so not to degrade or disvalue women, but rather to insist on doing things in proper order within the churches.

The Bible never condones or endorses misogynist or feministic thoughts and behavior. However, the Bible does teach on the importance of gender and their roles (see previous question). Men are to be servant leaders, which includes being the spiritual leader of the home. For Paul to bring up the "the law" in 1 Cor. 14:34, it is safe to ascertain he was referring to the Mosaic law and the book of Genesis as both give instruction on proper, biblical gender roles. Furthermore, if Paul is urging proper behavior in the church in regard to the Old Testament law, something must have been going on in the churches of Corinth that was contrary to the law. What was the problem? It seems in this case the women in the churches were causing disorder, division, and confusion by speculating the teachings of the church or proclaiming things contrary to the teachings of the apostles. Given Paul's concern for order in earlier verses, it's not a stretch to assume these women were not only causing confusion in the church, but were usurping the role of the man as the spiritual leader of the home. Paul not only expressed concern for proper order in worship services, but for the understanding and practice of proper gender roles within the home. He gives a similar instruction in his letter to Timothy, "A woman should learn in full quietness and submission. I do not permit a woman to teach or to have authority over a man; she must be quiet (1 Timothy 2:11–12)." Paul continues this line of thought by reminding his readers of the deception of Eve and the failure of Adam to protect his family from Satan's trickery (1 Timothy 2:13–15). Paul's two desires were to enforce biblical gender roles and to promote proper order within corporate worship services. In no way was he trying to keep women completely silent or treat them as inferior.

# CHAPTER 6

# HEAVEN AND HELL

## What Happens to the Lost When They Die? Do They Go Straight to Hell?

Everyone wonders what will happen after they die. As Christians, we hold to the biblical teachings on Heaven, Hell, and judgment. We know the Bible teaches that those who die in Christ will spend eternity with him and those who do not will spend eternity separated from God's love, grace and mercy in a real, literal Hell. Paul teaches in 2 Corinthians 5:8 that for the believer "to be absent from the body is to be present with the Lord." Jesus and Stephen both verbally committed their spirit into the hands of the God upon their death, and Jesus promised the thief on the cross that on that day he would be with him in paradise. However, the question remains. Do the lost immediately go to Hell or do they go to Hell after the judgment?"

Before we can answer this question, let me advise that the Bible doesn't give a clear, detailed timeline or sequence of events as to what exactly happens to a person after physical death. However, Scripture does provide some insight into the fate of the lost. First, we have to take into account the parable of the rich man and

Lazarus (Luke 16). . Even though Jesus was not exactly teaching on the nature of Heaven and Hell as the main point of this parable, it is unlikely that he would mislead his hearers about Hell. In the parable, the rich man dies in his sin and is immediately in torment The rich man is so hot he begs for a drop of water to cool his tongue. So from this we can ascertain that punishment is immediate. However, we need to keep in mind that the New Testament does distinguish between the two Greek words: "Hades" & "Gehenna." "Hades," according to some scholars is the place where lost people go immediately after death, with "Gehenna" being the place where non-believers go after the ultimate judgment of humanity as recorded in Revelation 19–20. The difference between these two has been compared to the difference between jail and prison; jail being the holding place until the trial is complete and then after the judgment is passed comes the prison sentence. Although these two terms are used, some scholars believe that these two terms are used interchangeably to describe Hell in general. Whatever the case, the fate of the non-believer is a place of punishment, separated forever from God's grace.

## In Heaven, Will You Get to See Your Family That Has Died?

People are curious as to what Heaven will be like, who will be there, and what will people do. Revelation offers glimpses of Heaven and some biblical passages give us an idea of what the afterlife will look like. However, on the whole the Bible does not offer a comprehensive view or a detailed timeline of what happens to a person when they die. Our culture today is interested, too. Countless movies, television shows, songs, and books focus on the afterlife and the metaphysical. Country music offers many songs about heaven, though sweet and catchy, offer poor theology. OK, to be fair every genre of music talks about heaven or hell at some point but country music seems to do so on a grand scale, most of the time speaking of grandpa and other relatives sitting on clouds pouring out raindrops and everyone they ever knew being in Heaven regardless of their standing with Christ. But I digress.

When most people discuss this topic, they do so based on conjecture and emotion. Now that is not to say that this isn't an emotional topic where some guesswork isn't involved but the Bible does need to be the ultimate authority here. Let's take a look at what the Bible offers on the topic.

I do believe the Bible indicates that we will see and recognize people in Heaven that we knew during our time on this earth. In the Old Testament, David declared that he would see his son again (2 Samuel 12:23). David seemed convinced that he would recognize his son in the afterlife despite the death of a child. The New Testament offers more on the topic as well. In the parable of the rich man and Lazarus, the rich man immediately recognizes both Lazarus and Abraham, calling them by name (Luke 16). During the Transfiguration, Moses and Elijah appeared and were recognized immediately by Peter, James, and John (Matthew 17:3–4).

However I believe the greatest evidence supporting the recognition of believers in the afterlife is Jesus himself. After his death, burial, and resurrection Jesus appeared in a glorified physical body. Mary recognized him at the entrance of the tomb. He even ate with his disciples and Thomas touched his wounds (John 20–21). Paul even records in 1 Corinthians 15:4–7 Jesus appeared and taught to hundreds of people after his resurrection. So, what does this have to do with us after we die? The Bible states that as believers when we die we will have the kind of body Jesus had after he rose from the dead (1 Corinthians 15:47-53; 1 John 3:2). It is then safe to assume if men and women in mortal bodies recognized Jesus, we will all be able to recognize one another in glorified bodies in Heaven.

## Pastor Noah, What Do You Think of the Movie Heaven is for Real?

To be completely honest, I have not seen the movie or read the book. Neither the book nor the movie offered any appeal to me whatsoever. Truthfully, I have no future plans to do see the movie or read the book. So admittedly I answer this question without comprehensive knowledge of the source material. I have been asked this question repeatedly and always get the same response from people. They want to know how I can answer the question without seeing the movie or reading the book. My response is simple: I don't need to. I believe I can answer the question simply by maintaining a biblical view of Heaven, Jesus, the metaphysical, and by being aware of the main synopsis and scattered details about the book/movie.

First off, I am going to operate under the assumption that the story is untrue. I know I cannot prove the story is untrue just as the little boy cannot prove the story is true. Therein lies the main problem: none of this can be validated due to the fact that it is a personal experience with no other credible source. There is no quantifiable evidence to support this claim. Scripture on the other hand has stood the test of time and was validated by many over the centuries. When God showed up in Scripture, there were witnesses to add credibility to the accounts. This is why the Old and New Testament hold up under scrutiny; hundreds if not thousands of people witnessed the events recorded within and therefore do not have to rely on the testimony of one person. Do you see the problem here? Let us not forget that Muhammad supposedly received the Koran from an angel while alone in a cave and Joseph Smith allegedly received what would eventually be the Book of Mormon alone in the woods of upstate New York. Less witnesses equals less credibility, or as in these cases, no witnesses equals no credibility. And yes, it has been pointed on that John was alone on Patmos when he received his revelation from Jesus but we must understand that John was already an apostle with apostolic authority. Due to his standing as an apostle, his writings contained nothing contrary to any other apostle and were accepted by the early church as authoritative. So don't go there.

Having heard sermons and read blogs about the book, I am convinced that the book adds elements to the afterlife that are not in the Bible. That, my friends, is **extremely dangerous ground**. To be fair and balanced, let's assume the story is true. If we operate under the assumption the story is true, it is still unnecessary. Why? For the Christian, we must understand the sufficiency of Scripture. That is, that God told us all we need to know in the 66 books of the Bible. Nothing else needs to be said. In fact, God's word itself states that it is sufficient for all teaching because it comes from God himself (2 Timothy. 3:16–17) and warns specifically not to add any extra teaching outside of Scripture (Revelation 22:18).

I am aware that holding this view will make me unpopular amongst some evangelicals but I urge you to consider one more passage of Scripture before you label me a cold-hearted party-pooper.

*Heaven is for Real*, like the countless other fanciful tales of near death experiences involving Heaven and Jesus which sadly fly off of bookshelves in record sales, fails to consider teachings from the mouth of Jesus. In the parable of the rich man and Lazarus recorded in Luke 16:19–31 we're provided a startling insight here that many Christians overlook. In the parable, the rich man is in agony while Lazarus sits with Abraham in comfort. The rich man, after begging for water to cool him off, pleads with Abraham to allow Lazarus to warn his family about the horrors of spending an eternity separated from God. This makes sense right? Surely the rich man was convinced that if Lazarus were to return from the dead and warn his family about the suffering he was going through, they would have no choice but to repent and turn their lives over to God. The plan was brilliant and foolproof. Surely this would work. However, Abraham's response to the rich man is both chilling and true. He replies to the rich man that his family had Scripture to guide them, which at this point would have been the Old Testament (Abraham refers to it as the Law and the Prophets). I can imagine how the rich man's jaw must've hit the floor. I am unsure as to what caused him more anguish; the fact that he ignored Scripture his entire life or that he knew his family was doing the same now. In one last desperate plea for his family, the rich man tells Abraham that if one goes back from the dead to warn them, they will repent. He reiterates his original request with intense fervor. Again, Abraham responds with his initial response instructing the rich man that his family has all they need to know in Scripture. He further tells the rich man that even if one were to come back from the dead, a supernatural event wouldn't convince them to repent if the truths of Scripture hadn't convinced them to do so already. This parable offers valuable insight not only to the destination of people after death but also the sufficiency of Scripture in all things, especially the nature of salvation. The Bible will convict and encourage people towards repentance, not stories of coming back from Heaven. In light of all this, I must take the position that even if *Heaven is for Real* is true it is unnecessary. Heaven is for real because the Bible says it is.

# CHAPTER 7

# VARIOUS AND SUNDRY ITEMS

## Church and State

*The following is an edited blog entry of mine from some time ago. I'm asked frequently concerning my views on how the church and state should interact, albeit these questions come from parents more than students. Instead of answering each question individually and thus producing overlap I chose to share this in hopes that it would present a more comprehensive answer.*

As an associate/youth pastor I have the privilege to frequent the public schools, especially since my wife is a middle school teacher and FCA sponsor. My heart is stirred with joy to see students live the Christian life, to hear them pray, and share their testimonies and struggles with one another. However, in our society there is much debate on how much the religious world should interact with the secular world. This particular example is merely an application and case study of how one views the wall that divides two entities: church and state. What is the nature of that wall? The answer to that question depends on whom you ask. Is it solid, allowing no interaction between the two? Modern society would have you think so as in some parts of the country those who dare mutter a word that rhymes with "Bible" are subject to an interminable blitzkrieg of lawyers and activists. Is the wall merely a rickety, dilapidated wooden fence with a swinging gate, allowing interaction between church and state with reckless abandon and total disregard for the consequences? Does the wall have nooks and crannies within the bricks and mortar that allow for limited and controlled interaction between two? I prefer the solid wall with the nooks and crannies. It seems the founders of United States did as well when they penned the Bill of Rights. Furthermore, America was discovered and settled largely due to the instability of the church states of Europe and their uncanny ability to trample on the rights of a person.

In order to present a good case for the third option, our wall with nooks and crannies, we must understand the dangers of the other two. Consider the first wall discussed...the solid wall and cornerstone of the impregnable fortress that is to separate all secular and religious life alike. Those who cling to this wall are prone to make outrageous claims such as " you can't legislate morality" or "Christians have no place in politics." These ideas simply do not hold water. In regards to the first argument that morality cannot be legislated I call their bluff and dare them to name one law (besides those kooky ones found in humor books) that do not reflect some moral thought of right and wrong. The only reason a law exists is because a society deemed something moral or immoral, which is morality in a nutshell. On to the second outrageous claim. The Constitution did not call for the full divorce of secular and religious life, but rather that the two should know their purpose: the church should be the church and the state the state. This in no way should discourage the religious person to be involved in civil affairs. Isn't it ludicrous to think that one's worldview and beliefs do not have an effect on how they live and interact with the world? The religious person votes in such a way that reflects their opinion, as does the atheist or agnostic. One view cannot be dismissed because it is "religious." In essence, people are always going to have convictions and are simply not going to transform into soulless, emotionless, robots when they live their lives. It is not as simple as merely flipping an ON/OFF switch. The atheist/agnostic is guided by their worldview as much as the next person. Furthermore, churches and government agencies such as schools oftentimes work together to alleviate poverty, educate, and meet other needs in the community. The wall is not solid. The Constitution forbids an established religious state, not the prohibition of religious activity and ideas in the public arena.

Here is where I will get in trouble: now that the secular folks have been examined, it is on to the Christians or theists in general... some of them anyway. The second wall described earlier was the rickety fence with a swinging gate, hopped by people, mostly well-meaning Christians with reckless abandon. Growing up in the South, the very of buckle of the Bible Belt, it is not uncommon to hear people make claims such as " we need prayer back in schools" or " school shootings are because the atheists took prayer out of schools." You are likely to hear phrases like these in church services that have forgotten what the true point of corporate worship is and have thus morphed their service into a Pro-America rally or a USO show. If your church service is indistinguishable from a Toby Keith concert, it probably should be examined. Back to the issue at hand: there needs to be a wall. The founding fathers were right in not allowing the government to establish a state religion. If you don't take my word for it, take a quick glance of church history from 315 AD through the Colonial period. When church and state are wed the results are terrible, catastrophic, and horrendous for both. Look at England in particular, when the common citizen could be executed because the next monarch was either Protestant or Catholic. Look at the Crusades, where "Christians" slaughtered people by the thousands in the name of Jesus because they wanted land, power, wealth, and the expansion of their empires. If you're not into history, just look at the world today. Many countries have not separated their church and state properly. As a result, people are persecuted by the millions as dictators oppose religious groups as they please.

Many Christians I know want to have their cake and eat it, too. These Christians have raised a fuss ever since state-sponsored prayer was abolished in the 1960s (which according to the Bill of Rights is in fact unconstitutional) and campaign tirelessly for prayer to return as it was in schools pre-Madalyn Murray O'Hair. But let the same Christian hear rumor of a Muslim or Hindu attempting the same thing. They literally panic. This is why state-sponsored prayer is wrong: a nation, which is not supposed to propagate and enforce a state religion, cannot force a child who is Muslim, Buddhist, Hindu, agnostic or any other religion to participate in state-sanctioned prayers to a deity in which they do not believe. Imagine what would happen if Christian children were forced participate in prayers to Allah or Vishnu as part of school? My guess would be civil unrest. The same set of rules must apply for everyone in a nation that did not set out to establish an official religion of the state.

At this point, you must be angered or perplexed by these remarks, or maybe a mixture of both. Rest assured that I am born-again evangelical Christian. I also love my country and have the deepest respect for the brave people who have served and still serve, giving me the freedom to worship freely and express ideas such as these. However, a great temptation many Christians have is to put too much weight in American politics. Take a trip back with me to the conclusion of Matthew's Gospel. People stood on a hillside experiencing the awe and beauty of a resurrected Christ. Jesus chose his words with careful precision just before he ascended from the Mount of Olives. We know how it goes: Christians are to go into all nations. The kingdom spreads by things such as baptizing, teaching, discipling, and trusting in the promise of Christ's presence even until the end of the age. Powerful words. A Great Commission...not a puny suggestion. However, it seems many Christians live as if Jesus had spoken something akin to the following:

*"Go therefore to your own nation to the exclusion of all others, after all that's the missionaries' job. Petition your congressman when something anti-Christian hits the news. Boycott, march and harass your lost neighbors until they see it your way, changing laws because that's the only way the kingdom can be made possible. Although you may find it hard to believe, when the guy you didn't vote for wins, I will still be with you."*

Again, let me reassure you that I am both a Christian and patriotic citizen. I believe Christians can and should stand up for issues such as sanctity of life and other moral issues. However, Christians should do this in a proper, respectful, and winsome manner. I would love to tell you that I am perfect at balancing this but unfortunately in my fallen nature I have failed. This is also complicated because nowhere in the Bible does one find a manual for how to interact comprehensively with the governing authorities. The Scriptures do provide some instruction regarding church/state relations in the life of the Christian. Jesus instructed the people to pay taxes to Caesar and also give to the Lord (Matthew 22:21). In the same vein Paul in Romans 13 encouraged believers to keep a strong testimony by obeying the civil authorities. However when reading the Bible I never recall Jesus or Paul instructing the church to place emphasis on the pursuit a religious state or lawmaking as a means of evangelism. This goes back to the issue of the church being the church and the state being the state. People are not going to be won to the kingdom of God because a law is penned in halls of Congress. The only way people will come to a saving knowledge of Jesus is by the work of the church; when God's people through the Holy Spirit work to pen God's law on the hearts of people. This is one aspect of our worship, which is the reason the church exists: to worship God. So at the end of the day I ask you to consider if the fact that state-sponsored prayers have been removed from schools even matters. Students still pray and are still winning their classmates to Christ. The Great Commission did not take a hit when prayer was "removed from schools." We could win all the wars in the political arena and yet lose the souls of men in the process if we lose sight of what is important. I have peeked in the back of the Bible and discovered that God wins in the end. In the meantime, let us love all and serve all.

## The Trinity

*Over the course of my time as a pastor I have received numerous questions concerning the nature of the Trinity. It is a difficult doctrine to say the least. It's difficult to explain because it is difficult to grasp. I spent the majority of my teenage and early college days explaining the Trinity in ways that I now look back on as insufficient and inaccurate. Implementing analogies (such as the solid, liquid, gas) seemed wise at the time but now present problems. If you are confused over the nature of the Trinity don't be alarmed. It is a doctrine that I don't fully understand and I don't think*

*I (or anyone) will until we see Jesus. Due to the length of my response I felt it necessary to put this topic in its own category rather than placing in the bullpen with the other topics. For purposes here I have organized my responses to discuss the Father, the Son, and the Holy Spirit in order. So with all humility (and I cannot stress that enough) here it goes:*

Perhaps no other doctrine found within Christianity has left me scratching my head more than the doctrine of the Trinity (or sometimes called "the Godhead"). While I by no means will have the definitive, end-all, clear as day teachings on the Trinity, I sincerely believe it is of the utmost of importance to have this discussion. Why you ask? If one examines the major Christian heresies of our day (Jehovah Witness movement, Mormonism, etc.) and the false teachings combated by the early church, you will find either a complete denial or gross misunderstanding of the Trinity, which often leads to a false, unbiblical view of Christ. The creeds of the early church fathers affirm that God is triune, meaning one in three, three in one. We as Christians do not worship multiple gods, but one God revealed in three distinct persons that share the same essence and being. Confused yet?

The word "Trinity" never appears in the Bible, although all three persons (Father, Son, Holy Spirit) are clearly seen and share a "one-ness" (John 10:30,16: 7–10; Colossians 1: 15–20). Let us not forget as well that the Father and the Spirit were both present at Jesus's baptism, giving us a picture of all three persons. Allow me to continue with a warning: explaining the Trinity can be a very dangerous endeavor. I don't know of any way to illustrate it. In times past I would teach it to teenagers by providing the example of liquids, solids, and gases. This is a grave error called modalism, meaning "in different modes." The example goes as follows: water is the same "stuff" whether it is shown as ice (solid), water (liquid), or vapor (gas). This illustration fails because in order for the illustration to be true to the nature of the Trinity, the solid, the liquid, and the gas would all have exist at the same time in the same mode.

I know. This material is difficult. I cannot even wrap my mind around it. However, I find deep comfort that I cannot. I am eternally grateful that God is infinitely beyond human thought. With that said, he has given us a peek into his character by providing the Bible and giving man the ability to read and think. Let us not be afraid to dive into the deep end of the pool. It's worth it. The more you learn about God the richer you will love, worship, and serve him.

## God the Father

When we hear the phrase "God the Father," our minds (well at least mine) are automatically drawn to the Old Testament. This is not a bad thing, as God chose to reveal himself the majority of the time in the Old Testament as such. God reveals himself to humanity as creator, sustainer, provider, all-powerful, all-knowing, omnipresent (everywhere at once), transcendent (above all we can imagine) Father.

Some names for God may help us further understand his nature:

**Jealous**- (Exodus 34:14) For us, jealousy is a problem and a sin. For God, it is as right and natural as anything. He alone is holy and above all things. There is no one or no thing like him. He has always existed (Genesis.1:1); creation is only here because he spoke it to being for his glory. No one or no thing deserves our praise and worship. We were created to love and worship him. If one has offense with God being a jealous God, it is safe to assume they love themselves too much anyway. If we get a grasp on who God really is this isn't a problem for us.

**El Shaddai**- "God Almighty; All Sufficient" (2 Corinthians 6:18; Revelation 1:8, 4:8) God does not need anything to exist. He has always existed, and is not dependent on anything to continue existing. He is above his creation, not a part of it. Similarly, another name for God, *El Olam*, means "the Everlasting God." He will always exist and he is outside of time and space.

**Yahweh " I AM"**- (Genesis 2:4; Exodus 3:14–15) This is the personal name for God. It appears approximately 6,000 times in the Bible. In the latter years of the Old Testament, the scribes would dare not write this name, but rather would take out the vowels (YHWH) or just substitute the word Adonai, which means "lord." God says all about himself that he needs to say when he uses this name while speaking to Moses at the burning bush. All that Egypt needed to hear from Moses is that "I AM" sent him. In fact, this name is taken from a Hebrew word that simply means "to be; exist, or will be." God reveals his glory by his very nature, by simply existing.

I have not even begun to scratch the surface of who God is. Who can? Volumes have been written for millennia and God still is so much higher and unfathomable than we can possibly imagine. Moses saw the backside of God's glory, a fraction of a fraction, and was awestruck beyond human words (Exodus 33:18–23). But thanks be to God that he has chosen to reveal himself in some ways:

through his word, creation, the Spirit, and his Son, Jesus Christ. (Hebrews 1:1).

## God the Son: Jesus Christ

The name of Jesus Christ is the most influential and controversial name ever to be uttered by human lips. The mere mention of his name brings peace, reassurance, and comfort to some. To others it brings annoyance, hostility, and hatred. Many claim that Christ was a great moral teacher and nothing more. However, C.S. Lewis wrote years ago that a man who said did the things that Jesus said and did could not be a merely a great teacher. But what did Jesus say about himself that made everyone pay attention to him, made his followers worship him, and provoke the Pharisees to execute him? For the record, "Christ" is not Jesus's last name. It is a title. It is from the Greek, meaning "Anointed One." In Hebrew, it is translated "Messiah."

Perhaps the most startling claim that Jesus ever made was to the Pharisees was recorded in John 8. At the end of this passage, Jesus mentions Abraham, the founder of the nation of Israel and whom all religious leaders in that time revered and honored. Jesus told them Abraham rejoiced to see his day, meaning that Abraham was happy when Jesus came to earth. By this phrase, Jesus implied intimate knowledge and fellowship with a man who had been dead over 1,000 years. The Pharisees responded in anger, reminding Jesus that he was only 30 years old, asking how he could know Abraham. Jesus responded, "Before Abraham existed, 'I AM'." When Jesus said this, the Pharisees tried to kill him on the spot. Does the " I AM" sound familiar? It is the covenant name for God the Father, Yahweh: the intimate personal name for God.

Two things are important to take from this account. First, Jesus is eternal. He has always existed and always will. In Revelation, he says three times he is the Alpha and Omega, which means he is the first and last, the beginning and the end (Revelation 1:8, 21:6, 22:13). Paul affirms that Jesus was present and took part in the creation of the world, and that creation was meant to give him glory (Colossians 1:15–20). This very issue here is what separates true, biblical Christianity from the heretical branches. Yes, I know in today's politically correct culture one is not supposed to say such things. However, as a Christian and as a minister I can do no other than speak what the Bible teaches. The Mormons and the Jehovah's Witnesses both teach that Jesus is a created being and is **not the same** as God. This is simply untrue and unbiblical. Jesus is not the created; he is the creator! Non-Trinitarian teachings also make an error claiming Jesus is not God, which cannot be true according to the New Testament. Paul mentions in Colossians 1 that in Christ the fullness of God dwells. Jesus himself claimed to be God by implementing the name "I AM," and accepting worship from his followers. He also used the phrase "Son of God," which of course does not mean a physical son (as the Mormons believe) but rather a term to describe intimacy and oneness with the Father. Early false doctrines in the church taught that Jesus was "similar" to God the Father. The true church stepped up at a place called Nicea in 325 AD to confirm that Jesus was the **same as God the Father.**

Out of all the doctrines of the Christian faith, the study of Christ (called Christology) is by far my favorite. I could spend 100 lifetimes reading, writing about, and studying Jesus and never scratch the surface of his majesty. John 1:14 reads that God became man, put on flesh, and dwelt among us. In all other faiths, God cannot relate to man with such firsthand knowledge. In Christianity, God knows what it is like to be a human being, with all the trials, temptations, pains, and emotions. He was tempted, but did not sin. He wept when he was sorrowful and laughed when he was happy. He fulfilled the law in ways we never could; he did it perfectly. Therefore, he was the only one worthy to be our Savior, the spotless Lamb sacrificed for the sins of the world.

One of the major problems concerning our subject matter that I have encountered in my various church experiences is this notion that the God of the Old Testament and the God of the New Testament are somehow different and should be separate. This is not true. The only difference is that in the New Testament, God became man and dwelt among us in human form (John 1:14). His attributes never changed, despite many within churches that claim that in the Old Testament God is all about wrath and in the New Testament he is all about grace and love. Neither one of these is correct. God by his very nature is unchanging, and Hebrews 13:8 reminds us that Jesus Christ is the same "yesterday, today, and forever."

To those who want to claim that God in the Old Testament was all about wrath, let me remind you that his grace and plan for redemption has been in place since before time began (Acts 2:23; Revelation 13:8). In fact, the first time man ever heard the Gospel is found in Genesis 3:15, where Satan is told the offspring of the woman would crush his head. Although this is the first time Christ is mentioned in the Old Testament, it certainly wasn't the last:

-Abraham is promised to have his descendants be a blessing to all the earth (Genesis 12:1–3).

-Jacob told his son, Judah, the Messiah would come from his tribe (Genesis 49:9–10).

-Moses promised a greater prophet than himself in the future (Deuteronomy 18:15).

-David is promised that his house would bring about the everlasting King (2 Samuel 7:1–29).

-The Psalms are loaded with references to coming Messiah (16, 22, 110 are the most notable).

-Isaiah foretells of a virgin-born King, and a Suffering Servant that will heal (7:14; 53).

-Daniel sees the "Son of Man," which is Jesus's term used to describe himself (Daniel 7:13–14).

-Micah speaks of deliverance coming from Bethlehem, David's hometown (Micah 5:2).

These are just a few places where Jesus is seen or spoken of in the Old Testament. The entire Old Testament points to Christ in some way. The entirety of it points to Jesus and his deliverance for mankind. Also, for those who think Jesus is all grace and love with no judgment or justice, think again. He tells the disciples that the inhabitants of towns that reject him will find it intolerable (Luke 10:12) and that division will come because of his words (Luke 12:52 –54). Also, the author of Hebrews tells us that if those who rejected the Law of Moses were punished, how much more so those who reject Jesus (Heb. 10:26–31).

## The Holy Spirit

The Holy Spirit is a person mostly ignored by some Christians and misunderstood by others. In recent days beginning around the 1900's, revivals centered on gifts from the Holy Spirit erupted in the Western United States, which serve as the roots of many church services today. On the other hand, the denomination to which I belong often lacks teaching on the Holy Spirit, either out of fear of being labeled charismatic or due to an overall lack of knowledge. Obviously, the most important factor to consider is what the Bible says.

The Holy Spirit is not an "it." He is a "he." He is the third person of the Trinity and is just as much God as the Father and the Son. The Spirit fully resides in believers at the moment of conversion and never leaves. His roles include glorifying Jesus (John 15:26; Acts 5:32; 1 Corinthians 12: 3; 1 John 4:2), providing evidence of God's presence (John 1:32; Acts 2:2–3), and guiding God's people by teaching and illuminating Scripture (Luke 2:12; John 16:13; 1 Corinthians 2:12.) Jesus promised that after he ascended back into heaven, a HELPER would come. The Greek word here is "*paraclete*", meaning, "helper", "comes alongside." In fact Jesus said that it is good that he ascend back to the Father, so that the Helper could come and effectively serve the church (John 14:15-31).

Most importantly the Spirit is submissive to Christ, which by no means diminishes any of his glory or authority. No person comes to faith in Christ without the Spirit drawing him or her to Jesus and revealing the truth of the Gospel to the heart. If you are a Christian today, the Holy Spirit courted you into God's presence and gave you the ability to respond to Christ. You could not have done this on your own, as we were all dead in our sins with no ability to do anything to please God. Thanks be to the Spirit who gave us the ability to accept Christ!

## Is It Wrong For Christians to Display the Confederate Flag?

*(I do not exaggerate when I claim this may be the most complicated and frightening question to answer. As I wrestled with this complex issue, I really couldn't find an absolute moral right or sinful wrong. I understand that this question and my subsequent response will entail more than a theological answer. This is an issue with political, cultural, and sociological ramifications that sparks heated debates and in many cases opens old wounds. My desire is to provide a proper biblical response and stay away from politics. I have my own views on social issues and how we examine the history of the American Civil War like everyone else, but my wish is not to make this response a platform for my political views. I do my best to approach this issue moderately and in doing so will probably offend both conservative and liberal people. I was almost done with this book when the tragic events surrounding the church shooting on June 17, 2015 in Charleston, South Carolina took place. Glued to the news for the next several days, I mourned not only the loss of my brothers and sisters in Christ gunned down while participating in a worship service but also the grave reminder of the racial tension that divides our country. After the Charleston shooting and the debate over the confederate flag in South Carolina raged, students in my youth ministry began to discuss the issue. Due to their willingness to discuss the issue I felt compelled to address it here. Perhaps the best way for me to answer is to share my story.)*

I was born and raised in the South. I was specifically raised in north Florida in a town called Hilliard, just north of Jacksonville

(Hilliard is the northernmost town in Florida on US 1 before you get to Georgia). In Florida we have a saying: "The further north you go in Florida the more south you get." That's true ... North Florida is sometimes referred to as lower Alabama or Georgia. I ramble about geography to let you know I was raised in a conservative, rural setting where it was not uncommon to see the Confederate flag displayed on a porch with a glass of sweet tea on the table. As a teenager, I identified as being a southerner. My accent is dead giveaway that I was raised in the south but no one would ever consider me a "redneck". Also in my teenage years I developed an interest in history, especially concerning the events that led up to the American Civil War and the war itself. I started reading everything I could get my hands on that dealt with the Civil War. In my room hung both the Union and Confederate battle flag. I even put a bumper sticker on the back of my Chevy pick-up truck displaying the Confederate flag with the phrase "Heritage, Not Hate" inscribed in the middle. I was aware of those who had used the flag to promote racist propaganda but since I did not hold their views I wanted to be sure that no one mistook me for a bigoted racist. I had a very good African-American friend in my youth group and another African-American classmate at school that never objected to my bumper sticker and Confederate flag T-shirt, even when I asked them about it. To this day I believe both would have been honest with me and wouldn't just tell me what I wanted to hear in order to avoid an argument.

Upon high school graduation, I began to work at a freight depot in Jacksonville. I was one of few Christians there and everyone knew I was preparing to attend a bible college the next year to begin my journey to be a pastor. One particular afternoon, an African-American co-worker noticed my Confederate flag sticker on my truck and asked me about it. I remember these words he spoke, *"Just be careful ... I wouldn't want anything to be misinterpreted. You're a good guy and you may mean well but not everyone shares the same opinion you do, Noah."* While this man didn't have a problem with it personally, he tried to explain it me from another perspective in a loving, kind manner. Looking back I wish I would've responded better than I did. When challenged on my assumptions, I became indignant: *"If anyone doesn't like it, its their problem. Why does it matter? I know I am not a racist and everyone who knows me already knows that. This is just what I do."* This was my first encounter with this issue but it would not be the last.

The following year I enrolled at the Baptist College of Florida to begin preparation for ministry. During the first semester of school a Caucasian student accosted me about my Confederate flag sticker: *"Man, you're a racist. You're supposed to be a Christian. I have black friends and that's messed up what you have on your truck."* I was enraged. This guy (whom had never met me before) was literally yelling at me outside the cafeteria. Clearly he was offended but did not articulate his objections in a winsome, loving, or reconciliatory manner. I must confess in situations like this my flesh has a tendency to take over (I never paint myself a saint and believe me I am painfully aware of my sin and shortcomings). Even though this brother in Christ was in the wrong for accosting me the way he did, I should have not retaliated with the same tenacity. Sadly, I did not respond with Christ's grace and I regret saying these exact words: *"Read a book and maybe you'll learn some history. Besides, I am from the South and I am not a racist. Maybe instead of shooting your mouth off you could sit and down and get to know me."* Again, let me reiterate that I am sinner saved by the grace of God in the process of my sanctification. That person's accusatory remarks were no excuse for me to fly off the handle. I never did apologize to that person and would like to take the chance to do so now.

I went back to my dorm that night still in a rage. My mind wandered back to the conversation with my African-American friend at the depot in Jacksonville. I marveled how the non-Christian friend at the depot could have a hard conversation in such a loving manner yet a Christian at a bible college yelled at me and called me a racist. I basked in my own righteousness as I thought about the Christian brother who had yelled at me hours earlier. Big mistake. God has a tendency of tearing down self-righteousness and bringing a person back to reality although it would not happen until the next morning after my New Testament course. As I got back from class that next morning I sat down to read the Bible for my morning devotional (or "quiet time"). I was in the book of 1 Corinthians where Paul discusses an issue that had been divisive in the Corinthian church. In the church there were some who were offended that some other church members would eat meat that had been used in worship of pagan gods. Paul uses the phrase "meat offered to idols." It was not uncommon in that day for worshippers of pagan gods to offer up food as a sacrifice in hopes of receiving a blessing or avoiding calamity. Some Christians would then buy this meat and use it for meals in their homes while others found this to be immoral and sinful. Paul explains that though eating this meat was not sinful in essence it could be sinful if done at the expense of another believer's conscience. In Corinth many new believers had at one time worshipped those false gods and for them to continue to eat the meat would make them feel uncomfortable or violate their conscience. Paul then urges those who would eat this meat to either refrain or do so quietly as to not cause an issue and to build up those brothers and sisters in Christ. Paul then wrote these words that struck me to my core: "Be careful, however, that the exercise of your rights does not become a stumbling block to the weak (1 Corinthians 8:9)."

Wow. Paul states doing something that is not sinful could be damaging to another believer. That caused me to evaluate my stance towards the Confederate flag. Even though I wasn't a racist and didn't see the flag as hate symbol, I could not escape the fact there were other Christians troubled by it. I could sit there and try to tell myself how wrong I thought they were but at the end of the day I was still offending other believers. I thought of my neighbor in the dorms, an African-American student. Did my stance on the Confederate flag offend him but his timidity prohibited him from telling me? Suppose he did say something. Would I respond with the same defensiveness, apathy, and anger that I had in times past? My mind began to race through scenarios and hypotheticals that I had never considered before. I felt conviction and shame not because I had worn a T-shirt or slapped a bumper sticker on my Chevy. I felt this way because I had willfully ignored the feelings of others, including my fellow Christians (and yes, including the one who yelled at me and called me a racist). As Paul closed out the eighth chapter of 1 Corinthians he gave a stern warning: "When you sin against them in this way and wound their weak conscience, you sin against Christ (1 Corinthians 8:12)." If I sin, I do so against Christ. Furthermore, when I sin in this manner the body of Christ suffers.

I was reminded of a verse I read earlier in Corinthians just days before, "'I have the right to do anything,' you say—but not everything is beneficial. "I have the right to do anything"—but I will not be mastered by anything (1 Corinthians 6:12)'." Granted in this chapter sexual sin was the topic at hand but the same principle applies. Just because I have the freedom to do something doesn't mean that I have to or that I should. I can do something and have complete freedom to do so but it may not be beneficial to me or someone else. The Holy Spirit used Scripture that day to break me of my sinfulness. I finished my devotional that morning with a prayer of repentance, thankful of God's forgiveness and second chances. Immediately, I grabbed a scraper out of my roommate's tool bag and removed the Confederate flag bumper sticker from that Chevy pick-up. I no longer wanted my allegiance to the South and my way of life to get in the way of my allegiance to the kingdom of God. If Jesus was going to be number one in my life I had to get rid of this potential stumbling block that could hinder me from being an effective witness (especially to African-Americans). Later that day I went to the store and bought a sticker to put in the back glass of that Chevy. To this day it remains and simply reads: JESUS.

Depending on how you view this issue you may be ready to throw this book in the garbage or send me words of affirmation on social media. I hope you understand that my decision regarding the Confederate flag is not a political one. For me it was an application of biblical wisdom that I couldn't ignore. My concern is for the lost world and fellow Christians, not political correctness. As I conclude let me offer a couple of thoughts. **First, if you are displaying a Confederate flag I do not automatically think of you as a bigot.** I understand southern pride and the history behind the Civil War. I do not agree with the politics behind the negative stigma that surrounds the flag in our modern culture. However, I try to be sensitive to the feelings of others on this issue. I know there are things that offend you. Things offend me, too. However, I cannot control if others are offended but I can control if I am being a stumbling block to others. Regardless of my feelings, I do not want to hinder my testimony before the world. **Second, I am not telling**

**you take down your flag.** The Bible does not command you to do so, therefore I have no right to tell you to do so. I do encourage you however to examine your life and the Scriptures carefully on all issues that are not so clear such as this one. Finally, I implore you to never let your allegiance to your culture or anything else take precedence over Christ and his commands. Being identified with Christ is much more important than heritage or politics.. Remember the words of Paul in Galatians 3:28: "There is neither Jew nor Gentile, neither slave nor free, nor is there male and female, for you are all one in Christ Jesus."

# AFTERWORD

Although this book is drawing to a close it is my prayer that it is not the end of your pursuit of the knowledge and wisdom found within the Bible. This project covered many topics but there are so many more questions out there for us as believers to uncover! Never stop learning. Seek counsel from trustworthy pastors, books, articles, etc. May this project be one of many tools used as you continue on your journey and let it be a resource for you when you are in the process of discipling someone else. Remember, growing in the faith should not just produce knowledge but also the application of the knowledge (wisdom). I hope it doesn't take you as long as it took me to differentiate between knowledge and wisdom. The desired result for the Christian is not to master the doctrines, but to use your knowledge to better live out your faith by making you a disciple-maker. Paul said it best when he claimed that if he knew it all but didn't have love for others, he had nothing (1 Corinthians 13:2).

The book of Proverbs begins by telling us that the fear of the Lord is the beginning of all knowledge (Proverbs 1:7). The word "fear" in that verse implies the meaning of respect and reverence. Maybe you have read this book and much of it didn't resonate with you because you don't know the God we have been discussing. If you have read this project but do not yet know Christ, I urge you to examine what the Scriptures teach concerning our sin, God's grace, and the work of Christ on the cross. I understand Christians will mostly read this project, but if you are not a Christian yet I urge you to take the first step of the journey with Christ. Turn away from your sin and trust Jesus. Commit to serving him the rest of your life and I promise you the journey may not be easy, but it will be worth it. It is surely anything but boring.

May God bless and keep you as you continue to serve him with all your heart, soul, mind, and strength.

# ACKNOWLEDGEMENTS

To every Sunday school teacher, VBS worker, small group leader, D-Now leader, camp counselor, and every other layperson at First Baptist Callahan who faithfully taught me the Word from childhood through adolescence...Thank You!

To my church family at Hardeetown Baptist Church– Thank you for entrusting me with your students, allowing me to serve you as an associate pastor, and for letting me work on this project. It is my prayer that this project is for your edification.

To my pastor, Tom Keisler– Thank you for your trust and willingness to let me help you shepherd the flock.

To my mentors in the faith and ministry, Lynn Hyatt, Todd Carr, Gary Holmes, and Derick Shepherd– your guidance over the years has no price tag.

To Jared Knight and Brandon Walls– For being the iron to sharpen this iron, you have my gratitiude.

To my brothers in the trenches of ministry, Rob Studstill, Josh Thomas, Alan Harmon, and Brooks Beike– This project is as much yours as it is mine considering our countless breakfast discussions.

To Jean Lamar and Natasha Drake– For instilling in me a love for reading and writing. Your words of wisdom are permeated throughout this project.

To my parents– Rick and Cheryl Raulerson, for taking Deuteronomy 6:4–9 seriously, which made immeasurable benefits for my sister and me.

To Jonah– my son who gives me so much joy, I am overjoyed beyond measure to be your daddy.

To my wife, Jennifer– You are the best gift I have ever received besides Jesus. You motivate me to achieve more than I ever thought I could. Thank you for being there and listening to me as I worked on this project.

Most importantly to my Lord and Savior, Jesus, who knew how to ask and answer life's toughest questions. Thank you for saving me.

# WORKS CONSULTED

Akin, Daniel L. *A Theology for the Church.* Nashville. Broadman & Holman Publishers, 2007.

Driscoll, Mark & Grace. *Real Marriage.* Nashville. Thomas Nelson Publishers, 2012.

DeYoung, Kevin. *What Does the Bible Really Teach about Homosexuality?* Wheaton. Crossway Publishers, 2015.

Grudem, Wayne. *Systematic Theology.* Grand Rapids. Intervarsity Press, 1994.

Gundry, Stanley N. & Steven B. Cowan. *Five Views on Apologetics.* Grand Rapids. Zondervan, 2000.

King, Clayton. *Stronger.* Grand Rapids. Baker Books, 2015.

Lewis, C.S. *Mere Christianity.* Oxford. HarperCollins Press, 1952.

Lewis, C.S. *The Problem of Pain.* Oxford. The Centenary Press, 1940.

Matthews, Kenneth, A. *The New American Commentary: Genesis.* Nashville. Broadman & Holman Publishers, 1996.

Piper, John & Justin Taylor. *Sex and the Supremacy of Christ.* Wheaton. Crossway Books, 2005.

Rae, Scott B. *Moral Choices.* Grand Rapids. Zondervan, 1995.

Printed in the United States
By Bookmasters